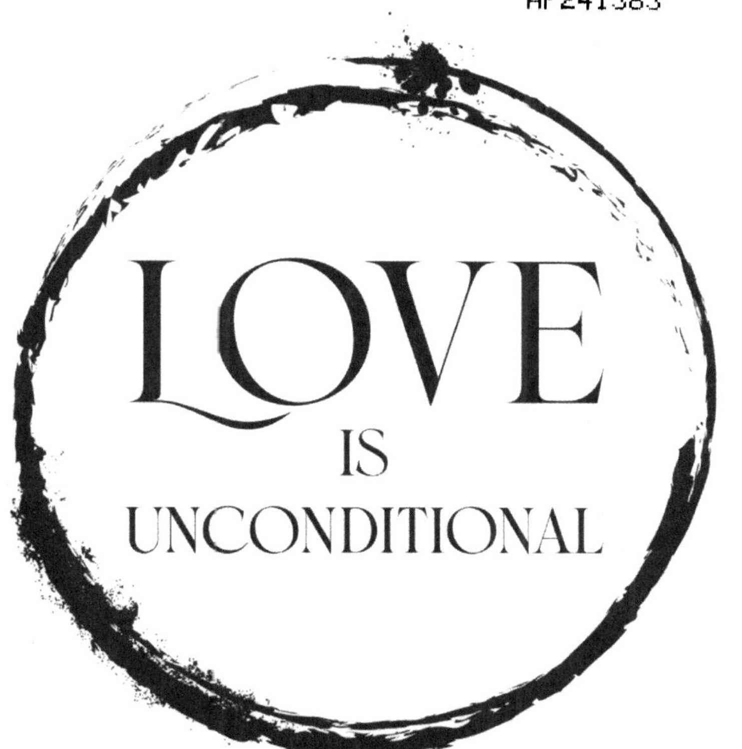

The Power of Your Purpose

Shelley Love, Ph.D.

LOVE IS UNCONDITIONAL

The Power of Your Purpose

LOVEstrong, LLC
PO Box 306
Owatonna, Minnesota 55060
www.drshelleylove.com
hello@drshelleylove.com

Paperback ISBN: 978-1-948806-08-4
eBook ISBN: 978-1-948806-09-1

Book Design by Transcendent Publishing
Edited by Mary Rembert

Printed in the United States of America.

*"The most beautiful people we have known
are those who have known defeat,
known suffering, known struggle, known loss,
and have found their way out of the depths."*

Elisabeth Kübler-Ross

CONTENTS

With deepest gratitude for everyone whom
I have encountered along the journey thus far,
and for your role in reflecting to me who
I am to become.

Introduction

I was born into a world that seemed to hold no love for me. Primarily critical, punitive, and conditional, the love I craved was fleeting. My earliest memories are of frenetic rages and stony silences, both of which made my blood run cold. I grew up in a home where the walls held more secrets than safety, and words were often weapons, not comforts. Abuse and neglect were constants that shaped my perceptions of life and myself.

For years, I believed I was unworthy, unlovable, and incapable of escaping the confines established by my upbringing. Those beliefs became my armor and my prison. Every harsh word and each absent embrace became bricks in a wall I built to keep the world out and myself in.

Life has a way of whispering to us, even in our darkest hours. For me, that whisper began as an almost imperceptible voice—a calm in the quiet recesses of my mind—and an unwavering presence in my times of greatest need.

Over time, the whisper became an insistent calling to look beyond the pain and into the depths of something greater. I didn't have the words for my experiences then, but now I know my connection with Source has been the only constant in my lived experience.

As I grew older, I faced life's trials with a blend of desperation and determination. I poured myself into learning, seeking refuge and escape in books and education. Despite being too young to fully comprehend the majority of what I began reading, I sought wisdom between the pages of books on human development, the mind, and family systems. My pursuit was not just an academic endeavor but also an act of survival—a way to understand the chaos that was my life and the world around me.

Yet, even as I achieved success on the outside, an emptiness lingered within. I realized healing wasn't just about understanding the mind; it was about connecting with spirit. This introspective awareness began a more complete unfoldment of my awakening—not in a dramatic flash, but rather as a series of quiet, profound moments that I now realize had been happening since I was a young child.

I started to see life not as a series of hardships to endure but as a canvas for transformation. I began to understand the pain I carried wasn't a punishment—it was a path. Each emotional wound held a lesson, a step toward reclaiming my power and finding my purpose.

This book is not just my story. It is a guide for anyone who has ever felt broken, lost, or unworthy. It is for those who seek to transcend their pain and step into their light. Through my journey, I have learned universal truths that connect us all—truths about resilience, forgiveness, and the boundless capacity of the human spirit to heal and evolve.

You are not your past or your pain. You are a spark of divine light, capable of creating a life filled with meaning, love, and joy. I hope the words in these pages will serve as a bridge—from your shadows to your light, from your wounds to your wisdom, and from your fears to your freedom.

Let us take this journey together. It begins not with perfection but with a single step. With each step, we walk toward the truth of who we are: limitless, luminous, and innately whole.

Welcome to your awakening!

PART 1

THE LIVED EXPERIENCE

"We delight in the beauty of the butterfly,
but rarely admit the changes it has gone through
to achieve that beauty."

–Maya Angelou

When Love Is Conditional

If life has taught me one thing, it is this: The why of what we do is as important, if not more so, than how we do it.

I spent decades hiding my truth, the reality with which I came into this world, and how I spent the first twenty-five years of my existence dodging the obvious. Self-medicating the emotional chasm within me with food, exercise, relationships, and even a period of what I now perceive as excessive alcohol consumption in an attempt to deny my past, appear normal, tolerate myself, and garner acceptance such that it was offered by those with whom I sought to align.

In the end, I was only hiding from myself. Well, in all actuality, I was hiding from the Divine being, which is me. Not just the physical me present before you, but the energetic me housed within the physicality of the body—Self in form.

All too often, individuals who place themselves in the spotlight of public scrutiny endeavor, consciously or subconsciously, to create a persona of apparent mystery. Known, yet not known. Seen, yet not seen. I do not question nor challenge their motivations for doing so.

In a way, I get it. For some, this becomes an almost primal drive that rises from deep within. Privacy and freedom to be oneself is a valuable commodity today. More so now than ever, it seems. Much of what occurs now was not an option when I was a child growing up in the 1970s and 1980s, and not just because I was a child. The world has changed drastically since then. The internet has forever altered how we give and receive information and interact, achieve, and relate. Gone is the perceived simplicity I experienced as a child.

While adulting has presented more challenges than I initially expected, it has also continued to grow exponentially year by year, with new layers added for every aspect of life, from aging and parenting to external influences that impinge upon the self. New and never-predicted challenges present almost daily, and with each passing year, I become increasingly invested in the simplicity of life.

My truth now is that I have spent most of this lifetime feeling unseen and unheard. Invisible. Rightfully so. I worked hard to keep the real me from being discovered—and it worked! Along with this success came the loneliness, isolation, and introversion one would expect. The pain of that, too, was almost too much to bear.

Of course, my inner dialogue created its own reality. Inevitably, I adopted the logical approach and believed hiding was the only way to protect myself from ridicule and questions, the scrutiny of which was too overwhelming to bear at such a young age.

As I got older, I confabulated an acceptable belief system that I was doing it all to protect my family and friends, even though the truth was I did not want to be rejected for being different.

In adulthood, the lies continued, and by this time, the inner dialogue had taken hold and was quite convincing. I had all but solidified my belief systems. Things morphed again, and it became about my chosen career's professional standards and expectations. Later, it became about protecting my children from negative appraisal and disparagement.

Certainly, no one could argue those well-thought-out and plausible reasons, least of all the me trying to get out and be free. The me attempting to live free from the confines of everything I felt imposing upon me. Yet, the lies I told myself continued, literally and figuratively, setting fire to the very truths I labored so hard to suppress.

Self-awareness and living one's truth are profound experiences. I encourage each of you reading this to seek that path no matter how arduous the journey. It is well worth the sleepless nights, the emotional turmoil, and the sifting through of the thoughts and feelings too numerous to expect along the way.

When you can look back over the lived experience and embrace it all while living your truth and knowing every moment led to where you now stand, self-contained in complete acceptance of those experiences and the self, it is absolutely priceless!

To that end, I choose to be an open book and share with you, the reader, a journey that transpired parallel to the lived experience, the unfoldment of which I have spent years deciphering from new and varied perspectives as I matured emotionally, intellectually, and spiritually. I have developed a profound gratitude and now recognize those foundational moments were crucial to the me I have become. While not the me I thought I would emerge as in adulthood, I can honestly say who I became is better than any version of self I could have dreamt into being. Long story short, I like who I am.

My personal journey is one of being raised in an environment of fear, void of the love and comfort a child craves, and one created to make me believe my value and worth were a conditional commodity. One based solely on how much I did for others and how well I complied with their expectations.

Despite it all, I now know every moment was a necessary part of the process. Each flickering in time, a thread woven into the tapestry that would become my life. I feel like a phoenix who has risen from the ashes. While this creates a dramatic picture, the intention is about the death (i.e., release) of that which no longer serves my best interest and the rebirth of self. I am grateful to and for all with whom I have shared the path thus far.

To know love as unconditional is not just a journey of the heart but also the infinite Self. It is a lifelong undertaking fraught with challenge, anguish, and losses often too great to quantify. So, too, it is a journey of inspiration, elation, and passion, the qualities of which are beyond the scope of language to adequately describe it. To know love is to find Self, even though the profound awareness of the lost self, in totality, arrives simultaneously within the precise moment of its discovery—irony at its finest.

Origins

Until the age of eight, I was one of four members of an intact nuclear family. Intact is not synonymous with being healthy. In fact, it was not. While the family unit was together, it was not a cohesive and nurturing environment. Father worked incessantly, partly driven by necessity and fully driven by his work ethic that commanded it. Mother experienced and expressed an inability to be effective in every meaningful area of life. My brother was in constant survival mode. I tried my best to be as helpful and compliant as possible while perfecting my ability to be invisible.

Knowing what I now know, I realize there were many reasons my father worked tirelessly for himself and others. The intrinsic reward of being physically busy was something Dad had known his entire life. Born to immigrant parents and raised on a remote farm in Ontario, Canada, he was no stranger to a hard day's work. He worked, too, to create and maintain social connections because my father truly enjoyed people. He thrived on being of service and developing creative ways to solve the perceivably unsolvable. An intelligent, thoughtful, and kind man, he was approachable, received well, and well-liked. It was who he was to the core of his being and now how others remember him—friendly, personable, and ready to lend a hand. He worked too, I think in part, to avoid the realities of home. Work and other projects were ultimately his passions and his escapes.

The long hours away from home each day created a conflict of their own, but this paled in comparison to the discord generated by the mind of my mother—a woman experiencing unmedicated and unmanaged severe and persistent mental illness. She was diagnosed with paranoid schizophrenia and manic depression, now known as bipolar disorder. At that time, more often manic than its opposite, and with the mania came an enhancement of her paranoid delusions that were unrelentingly all-consuming. The woman he left to care for his two small children, my older brother and me, had become almost unrecognizable to Father. Even less so to us, his children.

From a very young age, I knew Mother was different. For as long as I can remember, she was more often than not oppositional, judgmental, critical, and harsh. We did not mesh energetically, and being in her presence was almost abrasively uncomfortable, like being swaddled in sandpaper, to be exact.

Emotionally, psychologically, and physically abusive, Mother was not a safe place for any child. Insurmountable dissonance and a disharmony of immeasurable proportions were created within me when I was forced to seek comfort from the very person who inflicted harm. Without the vocabulary and emotional intelligence necessary to successfully navigate her daily outbursts, I instinctively went within. My soul bound in the frail physical form it inhabited, the innate light of my spirit dimmed. I shut down in the face of adversity and detached from the emotional and physical pain she created. Self-preservation became my way of existing. I later learned depersonalization, derealization, and dissociation are trauma responses. As a child, it was my normal.

I created a safe place within myself where there was nothing but love. I did not play out my reality; instead, I reinvented it. Mother isolated us from the outside world as much as possible, mostly due to her explosive behaviors and overall odd manner of being that she knew drew attention.

Left to my own devices, I created imaginary friends with whom to play and who provided much-needed comfort and support. I escaped frequently into a world of make-believe, where my dolls and stuffed animals became the family I did not have. Through connection with my soul-self, I learned how to be compassionate. Mirroring interactions I had observed between other mothers and their children, I cared for my dolls as I wished to be nurtured. I learned, too, by observing my father and how he interacted with my mother. Regardless of how she showed up, he was the ever-present calm and steady voice of reason. I do not recall ever hearing my father raise his voice toward her and never his hand.

Our annual family vacation to visit my father's side of the family in Canada offered a welcome reprieve. Mother was often more easily managed outside of our nuclear unit. Well aware others were observing her, she was wise enough to attempt to keep herself in check and endeavored to do her best. Daily rants generally resulted in her absenting the situation rather than the usual verbal and physical attacks. This was a great relief as I got older. My public humiliation awareness, as I call it, came into being around the age of five when I began having regular exposure to others through school. And so, Mother's oddities became less and less acceptable as my awareness developed.

As I grew older, school became my safe haven. I made friends, ate nourishing meals, and escaped the daily harshness and abuses dealt by my mother. I thoroughly enjoyed learning and the ability to connect with other children.

Truth be told, what I enjoyed most in elementary school occurred in the second grade. My teacher read to us during quiet time while we sat or lay on the floor near her. During one of these moments, I remember feeling safe for the first time. Subconsciously, I knew I wouldn't be unexplainably yanked from my place or kept awake by Mother's relentless yelling. I relaxed mentally. It felt safe to sleep at school. I relished quiet time and took full advantage of everything it offered. Unfortunately, I was usually so exhausted that sleep overtook me almost instantaneously, although I fought hard to stay awake, for I so enjoyed the stories.

Time away from home attending school became the sunshine in my otherwise dank existence. It was my emotional, mental, and physical escape from life. I thrived on the praise of my teachers and enjoyed being around my peers. The reprieve offered by school led to a sense of deep connectedness, and I craved the positive attention. My passion for learning is rooted in, instilled by, and reinforced through the many amazing teachers I was blessed to encounter as a small child.

My love of school did not come without consequences. I feared criticism and retribution from Mother, who punished equally for doing well and for not completing things to her expectations. It seemed she was jealous of the teachers' relationships with me. When I spoke fondly of any teacher, I was met with criticism and rejection that often culminated in my being told to go live with that individual, followed by violence.

Unseen

As a young child, I learned to straddle the margin between love and fear like an expert tightrope walker. I became skillful at not being seen. Assigned the role of scapegoat by Mother, I independently adopted the role of being my father's savior. I did not join my mother in her tirades against him; rather, I stepped in as a means of distraction and to offer a buffer in hopes of alleviating the many daily abuses he endured that were thrust upon him.

While my father was not perceived as someone who could protect me from my mother, he did not thrive on conflict as she appeared to do. He did not yell and never raised a hand to her, not even to protect himself from her physical attacks. He was our savior and yet not a savior at all. It's hard to believe my father convinced himself the abuses were only aimed at him when evidence to the contrary was presented almost daily. Although I have trouble understanding this reality, I accept it as my truth. Believing otherwise does not change that things happened as they did, and I do not need to understand it to accept it. Lamenting changes nothing.

Looking back with the analytical mind afforded me by the experience and maturity of adulthood, I now know my choice to align with Father was, in part, self-preservation. If he were forced to abandon us or chose to leave the family, we would be left to bear Mother alone. Abused children are often forced to choose between caregivers, align with one, or go against the abuser.

My brother rallied against Mother and began to fight back physically early in his second-grade year of school. I was in kindergarten when her abuses toward me became more frequent and intensely violent, and my brother endeavored to protect me, such that he could, and to take me along that path with him. I knew, or at least I believed, that I had no real escape. I begged him not to engage with her, to hide until she tired, and to apologize and make things better—for his sake, for all our sakes. Understandably, he had had enough. He was willful and stubborn enough to dig in, no matter the cost. The price was always high.

The relationship with my brother was what I believed was a typical sibling connection, such that I could even ascertain what that was as a small child. We were rarely around family or others with children our age. I had no template for comparison or measure of what constituted healthy or unhealthy.

He was my primary playmate and witness to the abuses I endured at the hand of Mother, and I was his. By the time we were in kindergarten and early elementary school, he had begun to change. Playtime and other interactions became increasingly strained. He began exhibiting attempts to control me and lashed out verbally and physically with increasing frequency. Almost daily, there were incidents of him hitting me, holding me down or otherwise restraining me, spitting on me, calling me names, and saying derogatory things—parroting sentiments from Mother whenever he became upset with me. He was persistently irritable, short-tempered, and often highly reactionary toward Mother and, more frequently, me.

I was confused by his increasing animosity toward me, although confused does not even begin to describe the impact my brother's personality change had on me. While I expected this behavior from Mother, his hot and cold behaviors were unnerving. I could no longer accurately predict how he was going to act. Sadly, this, too, was lumped into the *more of the same category* that was my normal.

My brother became increasingly sullen, brooding, angry, and explosive. It started in small ways—spilling a glass of milk, being sassy, dropping a plate intentionally, or refusing to do as instructed by Mother.

As the frequency and intensity of her abuses escalated, so did his behaviors. Acts of open defiance and running away became commonplace for him. Slamming doors, throwing things at Mother, hitting and kicking her while being abused, and screaming profanities at her was the new norm—part of the routine. In time, these hostilities were also directed at me.

Although he more frequently treated me like she did, my brother would step in and defend me from Mother's verbal tirades and physical attacks. For the most part, he provided a good distraction at best.

I once perceived his acts of defense as heroic. Perhaps to him, they were merely a manner of retaliation for the abuse Mother perpetrated against him. I honestly don't think he knows with any amount of certainty. Try as I may to see him differently, I could not resolve my reality that he, too, had become my abuser.

As children, we only know our normal until exposed to perceived similar parallel systems; then and only then do we begin to compare our family unit and others. Until this point of comparison presents, we are left to derive conclusions based on our family's interactions.

While there were shows on television (*The Brady Bunch*, *Little House on the Prairie*, *The Waltons*) that depicted what television normalized as a healthy family unit, these did not mirror my family experience and were perceived by me as entirely implausible. I had decided I could not survive in a family of that nature. The anxiety over waiting for things to erupt would be too great to manage, and I thought I would surely come undone. All too often, I imagined what really happened in those homes when no one was watching. While I understood it was television, I believed the depictions were of real families having real lives and did not think for one minute this was "normal."

For many, exposure to family constellations and peer groups other than one's own can be a confusing, albeit enlightening, experience. It certainly was for me. I remember standing in my neighbor's basement as her mother approached to discuss our tidying the play area in preparation for lunch. It was the summer between first and second grade. I was seven, and for the first time ever I was allowed to play away from home and with a neighborhood child. We had just moved to Minnesota from Idaho, and the neighbor girl was my new friend!

Despite her mother's questioning, we continued to play as we cleaned up, and we did not complete the task to her mother's specifications. Her mother approached again, with the same direction, and this time stated that if she did not follow instructions, I would have to leave. Her mother explained that the privilege of having a friend over requires meeting her expectations to follow the rules.

I burst into tears, believing that surely my friend was going to get physically punished the minute I left. I begged her mother not to hit her and offered to clean everything up myself before voluntarily leaving and never coming back. I was horrified at the thought of what I had brought to my new-found acquaintance. If only I had done as I was told, none of this would be happening. My mind raced ahead to make the situation better, to resolve it somehow.

I was attempting to rescue my friend from what I believed would be a certain harsh punishment. I can still see the look of horror on her mother's face as she attempted to make sense of it all. She reached for me, for what I now know was to connect physically and comfort me. I misread her cue, swatted at her hand, and screamed, which prompted the father to appear in the basement. It took some time for them to calm me. They then took the time to explain that their girls do not get hit but rather receive consequences that result in items being taken away or a time out from activities, early bedtimes, and so on.

It was all as foreign to me as I was to them. We didn't speak the same emotional or energetic language. As teachers in a small midwestern town, I am uncertain how much family violence these people were exposed to before we moved in next door. I know they frequently heard my mother yelling at us and our cries for her to stop hitting us. It was unavoidable, especially during the long, hot summers when windows were opened to relieve the heat and humidity looming everywhere.

Harbinger

The summer after third grade, things became undeniably interesting. Summers were horrid. I was cut off from the outside world. Worse yet, I was trapped at home with Mother! That summer was different—endless in a way I had not quite felt before. Mother's tirades became more frequent and increasingly violent. She terrorized me on an almost daily basis.

Shortly after school ended, my then 10-year-old brother was put on a bus to Ontario, Canada, in search of our father, who had disappeared weeks earlier. A few weeks before Father's disappearance, Mother chased him down the driveway with an ax, and he was ultimately jailed despite never raising a hand to her. Ultimately, my father lost his job and left town in search of work. Unbeknownst to me, he had settled in northern Minnesota after securing work for an iron ore pellet-producing factory. Mother knew and said nothing.

Around mid-summer, Mother managed to lose the house, and we were once again homeless and on the move. She was in rare form. After deciding to reconcile with my father, she brought me to the Iron Range of Minnesota, where we lived in a tent for most of the summer.

Eventually, we moved from the campground to a very small house and trudged through the remainder of the summer.

Things seemed to find their groove. Only the location was different. There was no escaping what life with our mother had become.

Before long, school began—another new school and the potential for new friends. This cycle had repeated frequently since my birth, and it was dependent on my father's work relocations. How I loathed being the new kid.

Shortly after the school year began, Father announced he was planning a driving vacation through Canada to Alaska in August of the following year. Father had always talked about seeing Alaska. For him, this was a dream come true. For my brother and me, this was a nightmare waiting to happen.

The thought of spending an entire school year fretting over the pending trip was unnerving. My brother and I concluded we could not endure it, and it must be stopped at all costs. Instead of happily planning the trip, we asked Father to divorce Mother. He was stunned! The questions that followed were answered justly yet with immense apprehension. If he did not believe us or, worse yet, told our mother, the punishments we believed would ensue just might be our end—or his. I still do not know how we managed to move beyond fear to where we stood in that moment, in the garage with the door locked, alone with Father and our truths. It was simultaneously epic and tragic.

What was to come next was an almost 18-month battle that began the day my mother was served with divorce papers. She lashed out verbally and physically against my brother, so he left the house, leaving me alone with her. He was injured after she hit him in the head with a hammer. I feared he would never return, or worse yet, that he would die!

Although worried about my brother, my focus quickly shifted to my survival. Mother was a different kind of "not okay" that day. I had never seen her so irrational and out of sorts, as we had come to call it, and it was all now aimed at me.

After what seemed like hours of her ranting, throwing and breaking things, and yelling threats against us all, Mother took a notepad and pen from our junk drawer in the kitchen and began frantically writing. She made me write several copies of the murder-suicide note she had drafted to my father. When I initially refused, Mother pointed Father's Colt 45 pistol at my face and said I was to either make copies of the note or he would come home from work and find me dead. She threatened to kill my brother next when he returned, and then my father.

I wrote the notes as instructed while Mother pointed the gun at me. She continued to yell about issues I knew nothing of and demanded answers from me that I was unable to give, which only fueled her rage. When the notes were done to her satisfaction, she instructed me to tape them in various places throughout the house.

Knowing I wanted to await my brother's return to ensure his safety, Mother manipulated me into leaving the house. She told me we were going to see Father at work and that my brother had likely gone there. Never did I imagine she planned to kidnap me instead.

We were located by state police several days later as Mother attempted to cross the border into Canada. Alone with my mother, who was completely unhinged at this point, and afraid I would never see my father and brother again, I did my best to do as she instructed and to be simultaneously invisible while hoping for the best possible outcome.

Terrorized for days, I believed I was going to be killed by my own mother. After what she invited and allowed to occur during our time on the run, I thought that perhaps my death would not be such a bad alternative to living with my new truths. Mother had become unrecognizable. For a woman who adamantly voiced her opinions about several areas of unacceptable behavior, she had stepped into the shadows, dragging me behind.

A child should not be exposed to intoxicated strangers or observe their mother engage in sexual activity. Mother may not have fully known what she invited, and at that point, I believe she could not rescue me from the men she chose to associate with. I knew my fate was sealed when she told them to keep me quiet. For weeks and months afterward, I grappled with what it all meant and found nothing that made sense. I was shrinking into myself to the point of disappearing.

The divorce ultimately occurred, and Father was awarded full legal and physical custody of my brother and me. He was only the second man in state history at that time to achieve this outcome. It was hard won. If not for my brother pleading with the judge, the result would likely have been different. The 1970s was not a time to acknowledge the father as a primary parent. Thankfully, the courts administered justice.

Mother did not go down without a fight, however. The divorce and all its legal proceedings took a toll on her mental health. She was declared unfit to parent and was forced to comply with supervised visitation. This was not a smooth or amicable process by any means.

Before the end of the year, she ceased to have any contact in person or otherwise. Mother had all but disappeared from my life, leaving behind the fallout of her relentless and varied abuses. Father was either too ignorant or too focused on survival to see that our needs for consistently available positive influence, unconditional love, and compassion were not being met.

We were left to struggle with the aftermath of a mentally unstable and abusive mother and an absent father. Neither of us fared well. In hindsight, perhaps Father was shell-shocked and knee-deep in his own recovery processes, but from where we stood, it did not appear he spent time focused on self-healing. I honestly don't think he knew how.

My brother's anger issues continued to grow, as did his self-reliance and fiercely independent nature. As his anger grew, the criticisms of me escalated. What scared me the most was his satisfaction from exerting power and control through intimidation tactics and threats.

I guess that is what happens when one is the target of unspeakable neglect and violence beginning in infancy. In all honesty, I understood how he became the person he was. I didn't like it, yet I found a way to accept it as the way he knew how to be—at least what had become comfortable for him. He had learned that love was a conditional commodity. His narrative and outlook were as bleak as mine.

Despite everything I was subjected to by my mother, the rejection, contempt, and intentional abuse from my brother was a new level of hurt. Safety was no longer found in his shadow, as it once had been. The realization that I was never safe had become the totality of my reality. There was no safe place or person in my home, and worse yet, I could not keep myself safe. This realization is the most profound emotional experience of my life to date.

I believe my reality holds no value in his experience of it all. I don't think my brother will ever view what he has done to me as damaging. In part, he is correct. On a soul level, these interactions offered an opportunity for both of us to learn.

From a human perspective—the lived experience—over time, I lost all respect for him. We had both survived the traumas and tragedies set forth by our mother, and the aftereffects of it all was our undoing. Our perspectives differ greatly. Whatever my brother's truth is, it will die within him. I know mine, which holds the most value for me.

Acceptance has allowed me the space to acknowledge his interpretations and all their trappings. At one time or another, we have both lied to ourselves to support a given narrative. It's called survival. Forgiveness of the situations I experienced has allowed me to know and express my truths. For that, I am grateful.

IMPACT

Perceived rejection, secondary to verbal abuse, is what hurt the most. While bruises and broken bones healed, words played a repeating loop in my head like an unyielding hamster wheel that continuously bled over into my emotional self and the perspective of who I was. I had determined there was no value in me as a person—for Mother, for Father, my brother, or anyone else—or so I believed.

To that end, I had become the self-fulfilling prophecy initially created by my mother. I was "worthless," a "nothing," a "thing that should never have been born." This was my truth and became the way I showed up in the world. I had a skewed and faulty template. Anything that mirrored or added to my lack of self-worth stuck to me like glue. I accepted it fully, embraced it as my truth, and actively deflected anything contrary, negating it with near-expert skill.

During the processes involving the divorce, residing at home with my mother was deemed unsafe because of the recent kidnapping at gunpoint incident and the numerous instances my brother and I reported to the police regarding her neglectful and abusive behaviors, the telling of which was like being gutted.

While purging years of countless incidents perpetrated by Mother against us felt like a release of sorts, I knew it was only the beginning of the spillover. Once I began speaking, I was afraid I would never stop—detail after detail flooded out of me like a spring thaw over a dam, no longer able to hold back the relentless torrent bearing down on its resolution. I remember one officer taking several breaks, clearing his throat repeatedly throughout our time together, and offering support and encouragement that I was safe—promising he would not allow those things to happen to me again.

When the judge learned of our reports, he determined we would not be required to speak against our mother during the closed court proceedings. Instead, he spoke with each of us individually in his chambers. The judge painstakingly went over each detail of our reports to the police and understandably had his own questions.

I remember being scared to tell the man anything, as I had been with the officer. Scared that he, too, would not believe us, that Mother would find out, and ultimately that things would not change. Through the cumulative hours of speaking with him, the judge was flat. Absolutely unreadable. I feared this was all for nothing and reverted to my safe place to be unseen. The narrative ceased, and I began speaking in one-word responses. I spoke only when spoken to and answered only yes or no. It wasn't until he asked if I remembered how far back the abuse went that the breach occurred, and I broke.

I was four years old the first time I remember Mother saying she wished I was dead. While my only reference point of death at that time was a family pet, I did not know what death meant for me. I knew by her tone and the violence she was inflicting that it was not a good thing.

I had been lying on the bed in my parent's room when Mother entered, yelling about something. I was too startled to make sense of it and was quickly yanked from the bed by the arm. She brought me to the bathroom, where the verbal out-lash continued. This was the first incident where she attempted to drown me to "get the devil out." There would be two such incidents that I remember.

Mother's active delusions were fixed, one of which was central to me and not in a good way. I explained to the judge how she believed I was my father's "lover" and this was the "devil" in me. I am not certain what chronological age she perceived me to be during these times, but this delusion was the precursor to most of the verbal and physical abuse I endured at her hand.

Some of this was so severe that, in one such incident, during the winter of my second-grade year in school, my brother believed she was going to succeed in killing me. After being locked out of the house by Mother, my brother, clad only in his pajamas, braved the barely above-freezing temperatures without boots or a coat and ran across town to bring my father home from work. While I remember the beginning of the incident, I do not honestly recall how it played out or ended other than regaining a sense of awareness while in the hospital several days later.

As a small child, I did not know what a "hussy" or a "floozy" was. All I knew was that my mother perceived me as her competition for my father's affection, and she appeared ready to end me to make it stop. I was ashamed to detail this to the judge, yet finally telling someone felt oddly good. The guilt of her accusations had nearly consumed me. Although I did not know what I had done, having her repeatedly tell me my father did not love her anymore because of me did not feel like a good thing. My only choice was to stay away from him when he was around. I did not want to invite unwanted attention from Mother. Sadly, I learned over time there was nothing I could do to avoid it. The reality of my mother's experience lived solely inside her head.

Having gotten lost during the telling of it all, at some point, I stepped in front of my shame. I looked up through the tears and sobs that had completely overtaken me, seeking some sense of reassurance from the judge that he understood the intensity of it all and how important it was that we do not live with Mother. Unable to read his blank expression, I imagined that to him, this all likely sounded like a Friday night made-for-television movie, such that they were in the late '70s. I knew how much Father abhorred lying and could only imagine how things might go if the judge perceived I was lying. He then asked what I believed my mother meant by her words and if she had explained any of it to me, and he asked about my relationship with Father. In hindsight, he was likely endeavoring to explore any truths to Mother's accusations. I still couldn't read him, which was unsettling in a completely different way. I provided the information he requested.

I remember feeling hopeful when the judge asked why I wanted to live with my father. He stopped writing and looked at me intently as I spoke. I knew this was a pinnacle moment and gathered all the courage within me. I scooted to the edge of my chair. Asking permission to speak, I looked him squarely in the eyes and bluntly stated I feared one day my mother would succeed in killing me, and living with Father was the only way to prevent it.

Tears welled in his eyes as he continued to look at me. I felt a sense of relief wash over me and remember thinking maybe, just maybe, he would help us all. A smart man, the judge queried further about why I said I would live with my mother despite everything I had revealed. I was forced to explain my contradictions.

Initially, I said if I went with Mother, each parent would have a child, and things would be okay. Not satisfied with this response, the judge encouraged more of a response, and I told him my truth. I related that although I wanted to live with Father, I believed if placed with him, my mother would kill him and my brother to get to me because I was her prize against Father. Not only would Father then be dead, but Mother would also be all I had left. The thought of that reality was unbearable.

While I was not present for my brother's day of conversations with the judge, I can only imagine their time together was spent detailing his remembrances of our mother's many abuses toward him. Some are too horrific to retell, even now.

Our time with the judge immediately resulted in an order to place us indefinitely outside the family home. Ultimately, we stayed with one of my father's co-workers. It was a busy house with a blended family—four children and two parents who appeared to struggle to relate to each other, almost as if they lived separate lives.

In this setting, I was exposed to sexually abusive behavior. I observed the man engaged in sexually inappropriate behavior against his adolescent daughter on an almost daily basis while the man's eldest son targeted me. Sadly, he only continued what had happened to me at the hands of the adolescent son of my mother's friend when I was only seven. This time, however, I did not keep it a secret as I was intimidated to do previously.

When I revealed the boy's behavior to the man's wife, my account of things was refuted, and my father became involved.

Although he questioned the situation and seemed conflicted regarding how to proceed, he apparently required assistance with our care and felt compelled to denounce my report so we could have a place to stay.

Unfortunately, I was told I was reading too much into the boy's actions and was making a big deal out of nothing. I was told that I had misread the situation, was seeking attention, and was ultimately not believed. Everything I said was dismissed as secondary trauma from the recent kidnapping events, which was used to sweep it all under the proverbial rug.

The abuse continued, and the boy persistently created circumstances by which to gain further access to me. We were forced to remain in this setting for several months. Unfortunately, I was unable to overpower or otherwise avoid him. Nothing was done to protect me, and without being properly addressed, the boy's contacts increased in frequency and continued until such time we were no longer made to reside with his family—almost one year later, at the finalization of the divorce when custody was granted to father.

Once we could return to our family home, life resumed some semblance of normal, if normal was having a father who was employed performing full-time shift work and holding two jobs on the side. He was rarely home to provide guidance or parent either of us. Our normal had shifted—not for the better or the worse—just different. Safety, as I perceived it was needed, was not established or provided consistently other than the food and physical shelter Father provided. We were inadvertently required to become completely self-reliant and somehow managed to rise to the occasion. Truth be told, we did not have a choice. We did not thrive; we existed.

Into the Fire

A few short weeks after returning home, an unpredictable event occurred that would forever change my sense of safety in the world. Father was working overnight, leaving my brother and me home alone as usual. On this night, however, an uncle was spending the night at our house. He was a man around whom I had never felt comfortable. Although I had no reason to distrust him, energetically something always felt off, and this night would be the culmination of my perceptions.

Sometime during the night, he attempted to sexually assault me. When my feeble endeavors to talk him out of it were not effective, I resorted to physically resisting and then fighting against him. For several minutes, it was as if time had stopped. Had my brother not been home, I fear the outcome would have been much worse than it was. Despite what he did accomplish, I was oddly more afraid of punishment from my father than anything my uncle could have done. Sadly, in a few minutes, this man's actions forever changed me.

Weeks later, when I finally mustered the courage to tell my father, I was immediately dismissed, accused of lying, and threatened with a spanking. When I persisted, Father consulted with relatives and, in doing so, related my account of the incident, which caused a gargantuan upheaval in our family system. I then became the liar, the one not to be trusted, the outcast.

The demise of my relationship with my father took another substantial hit. What he did not comprehend was that my respect for him took an even bigger one. He was no longer my hero and protector—a loss I mourned until the time of his passing nearly two-and-one-half decades later. The culmination of these events and the consequences that followed inadvertently conditioned me to question everything I believed true, at least to that point.

As if things couldn't get worse, they did. One year after the divorce was finalized, our lives were forever changed. That's when Father began his search for companionship. He ultimately decided on a twice-divorced woman who had five children. She was engaged when they met, which quickly fell by the wayside as Father spent time repairing her various appliances and vehicles and performing other odd jobs around her home.

Neither my brother nor I could see the attraction to this situation, and we certainly did not invite nor welcome their togetherness. Despite our objections, the relationship continued. Father became overly involved in their lives, so much so that much of his time away from work was spent at their house. Situations unfolded early on that drew a line and sides were chosen. Rejection and feeling loved conditionally presented again and again, year after year, in what would become our relationship until the time of my father's passing over 20 years later.

While I thought life had been difficult up to that point, it had all just been the appetizer, and the full course was about to be served. When my father allowed me to begin dating, I had a short-lived, father-approved beau in the ninth grade. My later choices and the one on whom I finally settled were not the most savory of characters, as Father would have put it.

Being indignant and quite protective of my dating relationship, I ensured it continued. Sadly, this also eventually led to my getting kicked out of the house almost immediately after school ended, following my junior year in high school. Although, if you asked my father, I was given the option to leave and made the wrong choice. This came on the heels of the previous summer, when, at age 16, I left home to reside with my grandmother and great-grandmother in Kansas. Unfortunately, due to her health issues and the need to provide care for my great-grandmother, I was unable to remain with her.

I returned to Minnesota, and the anguished relationship with my father picked up where it had left off, only now he was more unyielding and constraining. Such that it was, home ceased to be a place of solace. Scared, alone, and lacking resources, I felt invisible to my father and society. Barely 17 years old, and I was homeless. Adolescent homelessness was not the epidemic in 1987 that it has now become. I was the only person in my high school who lived independently of a parent or other guardian, and the school proved to be less than sympathetic to my circumstances.

Completely unaware of what to do next, I spent the first night at my then-boyfriend's house, with his parent's stern warning that I was to leave in the morning. I refused to return to my father's house because that would mean defeat, and I was, at the time, far from defeated. I slept in a friend's car for several days, then couch-surfed a few more with a pregnant friend of ours with whom my boyfriend later cheated. I stayed with him, clinging tightly to any lifeline I perceived as viable. Bad decision.

My non-plan of existence was temporarily delayed when my father had me arrested as a runaway, and I was detained at a juvenile crisis facility. Although this was his attempt at forcing me to return home, it did not work. In fact, it backfired. I became increasingly indignant. In this placement, some services became available, and I was ultimately sent to an emergency foster home while negotiations continued in attempts to make me return to my father's residence.

I resided with the wonderful family of a boy with whom I attended school. He had the kind of family I had always dreamed of—several siblings and parents who were present and who expressed love, abundant laughter, and a true sense of family, such that I believed it should be.

Father continued to produce roadblocks to my independence, and I became increasingly unsettled with my circumstances. After a few weeks, I left the foster home to reside with a school friend and her family. I shared her room and bed; although not what I ultimately desired, this was one step closer to not being controlled. Although her father was a bit too handsy for me to feel comfortable, I learned to stay away from him and keep my mouth shut. I endured what was necessary to make this placement last long enough to implement my plan.

Once again, school had become the only constant in my life. I acquired a job, then two. I petitioned the courts to become an emancipated youth. Once emancipation was granted, I submitted an application for an apartment and quickly secured my own residence. Things were looking up!

Unfortunately, my drug-addicted and all-too-comfortable-with-criminal-activity boyfriend decided my place was now his as well. I received renter's assistance and food stamps, which I endeavored to remove myself from as soon as financially feasible. I did not own a vehicle. The school bus provided my morning transportation, and after school, I walked several miles to work and then later home. Winter presented harsh circumstances, but at least I was self-sufficient for the most part with the help of public assistance monies.

Weekends were spent working and catching up on homework. I was determined to graduate. Although I was absent from school frequently and was required to make up hours for the time missed, I managed to consistently earn a placement on the honor roll, an accomplishment of which I am still proud.

Life was unstable at best. My boyfriend's infidelities and disrespect continued. In fact, it became progressively worse, as did the drug use and behaviors with his criminal associates. His illegal behaviors skyrocketed to include the sale of various substances, trespassing, theft, and his arrest for indecent exposure at age 17. Sadly, fear insisted I stay paralyzed into submission and go against every voice screaming in my head to leave. By age 18, he was dishonorably discharged from the United States Air Force and attempted to resume life as it had been before leaving. Thankfully, I was unwilling.

He continued in a downward spiral of alcohol and substance use and criminal behaviors. He engaged in the repeated sexual abuse of a 13-year-old girl whom he entrapped into a dating-type relationship even though she was unable to consent to anything with a 19-year-old man. Her parents were clueless. When I told them of the situation, nothing was done to intervene, and they merely forbade her to see him. Sadly, their situation continued until running its natural course.

He was not the first to be unfaithful, and he would not be the last. The blinders did not come off until after I spent six years with a man who was involved with another woman off and on for the entirety of our time together, and others, too, I was told. Sadly, his alcoholism and infidelity ended our marriage, and he later married the woman with whom he had primarily been cheating. Over 25 years, she has endured a relationship with him. Good on her for staying the course, for whatever reason. I wouldn't wish his behavior on anyone, not even her.

In the working-through process, I discovered that perhaps I was emotionally absent from the relationship or at least not as physically available as he would have liked. I was driven to achieve, and attending college full-time while working three jobs was a bit of a stretch. My attention was diverted, and I missed some important cues—mine and his. Maybe, just maybe, I did not want to see it for what it truly was. I was afraid of what it would mean about and for me.

While I like to think I was present and keenly aware of life at that time, I now know I was not. At least not to the degree I am now capable. I know I loved with reckless abandon, with everything in me, and I trusted him implicitly, and for the opportunity to do so, I am grateful. I also know that love can be truly blind, and when mingled with years of trauma and an absent sense of personal value, I was the perfect storm.

I would like to say I never think about those years, the situations that transpired, and the what-ifs of a young adult attempting to build a life. So too, wondering how it would have all played out had things been different for me. The reality is that everything happened the way it was intended. I have created a blessed life, not despite that relationship but rather because of it. I cannot say the same for her. Unfortunately, she has spent the entirety of their marriage being the other woman.

I am appalled my younger self did not see through the abuses I endured or the rationalizations spewed to justify my reported unworthiness of love. Sadly, I believe it was self-preservation and for the sake of retaining relationships. Moreover, I did it out of fear of rejection and abandonment. I had learned that loving me was conditional, based on my assigned value and the worth others chose to bestow. What I did not know then was that my worth existed independently of the opinion of others.

Looking back, I was surviving, and it was a meager existence. While there were many things over which to hang my head, I was proud I did not succumb to the sheer terror of being homeless. It pushed me to discover a drive and resourcefulness I did not know existed.

I am most proud of graduating from high school, and although I took a year off to recover—what they now call a gap year—I attended college afterward, and my education culminated in earning a Ph.D. in Clinical Psychology. I may not have known much back then, but the many wisdoms my father had passed on became my guiding light. Although he often thought I wasn't listening, I heard every word. Father valued education and frequently said, "They can take everything away from you, but they can never take your education." His statement was pretty accurate for a child of immigrant parents who survived the great depression, a man whose third language was English, which he learned in school as a small boy. Father was spot on!

Father was right about many things, more than I could recognize or appreciate most of my life. Thankfully, the opportunities for personal growth allowed me to get out of my way and see him in a different light. Although I still do not agree with many of his choices or methodologies, I can now appreciate his efforts. Father did his best, given who he was and what he knew. I am certain if he had another chance, several things would be different. At least, I would like to think they would. The outcome of that is for another lifetime to determine.

FRACTURED

fter 19 years of dating the woman with five children, my father finally married her and then died four short years later. Their relationship imposed several challenges on our nuclear family; the scores are too many to detail here. Suffice it to say, my father believed he was happy, and he felt loved. That was important to him.

I, on the other hand, felt abandoned repeatedly as a child and well into adulthood. Our relationship remained strained until his death, and then an unexpected and different kind of loss experience surfaced. While I had continuously grieved the loss of his presence while he was alive, it was nothing like grieving my children's grandfather and the man they would never get to know. The sands of conditional love slipped with finality through my fingers, and I had yet to recoup all that had been lost.

Sadly, the unwanted abuses of childhood weren't to be my last experiences of someone believing they could do what they wanted to my body. Since my uncle, the sexually inappropriate behaviors against me continued. Unfortunately, later the same summer as my uncle, it was a neighbor man and then his nephew. In high school, it was an obsessed and controlling boy I dated a few times, who was imprisoned two years later for attempted double murder. I guess I was let off easy, considering what he would become. Lastly, it was an adult male co-worker. When I reported the co-worker, the store manager told me, "I brought it on myself." Honestly, I was completely unaware the man was in the room until he grabbed me. Again, with the conditions regarding my worth and value, how much was I expected to endure?

Despite my hypervigilance in such situations, the inappropriate sexual contact and assaultive behaviors against me continued. As an adult, the stranger contact ceased but it then became those closest to me: an intimate partner, his trusted friend, my intoxicated spouse, and a partner who took advantage of the situation while I was heavily under the influence of pain medication following surgery.

I had come to believe I had bad radar for these types of people, or perhaps I had put out a vibe that they thought made it okay. In any event, I had almost come to expect it. I most certainly did not feel compelled to tell anyone. After all, I was taught no one would believe me, and I would get blamed, that the behavior was to be expected, and girls/women bring it on themselves, and to roll with it and just let it happen. As one man put it, to "not be so uptight." This was yet another example added to the pile of reasons why I was damaged goods, which for me equated with not being worthy of love except in the ways that served what they wanted.

These events shaped my reality of self, my worth, and my value, and ultimately, what I believed I deserved in relationships with others. The scaffolding of what was to become self was built upon quicksand.

I have since worked with male and female sexual predators for over 22 years in one capacity or another (i.e., state and federal prisons, civil commitment programs). I no longer excuse their behaviors or rationalize mine.

Isn't it interesting, though, that my life's career has been spent engaging in interventions with individuals like those who had caused what I believed to be irreversible damage? That said, I continue to learn and grow personally and professionally. Each day brings new challenges, and I am better equipped to manage them, having already crawled through fire. After all, I am born from the ashes of my soul's doing, exactly the way it was intended.

Several times during early adulthood, I attempted to reconnect with my mother. Of course, her attempts to force a connection by coming to my work to harass me when she was in town or by calling the police to conduct welfare checks did not win her any favor. That was, for me at that time, humiliating.

Mother married for the third time when I was 19, and we spent the better part of one day together. He was a passive, polite, and unassuming man. I wondered if he knew what he was getting into. I saw her again for a few hours when I was 21 and a couple of days later that same year. It did not go well. She was out of touch with reality and ramping up to a full-blown psychotic episode.

When I was 25, my mother briefly appeared at the hospital following my father's first cancer surgery and was quickly escorted from the premises and luckily avoided arrest for her out-of-control behavior. This was the last time I saw her.

The last time I heard my mother's voice was when I was 28. She called the small country hospital in Kingman, Kansas, as my maternal grandmother lay dying. I answered the phone, gave her explicit instructions, and listened as she made her peace. The call ended without incident. Mother was alone, unable to travel to see her mother, and would never see her again. My heart ached for her. I could only imagine what she must have been experiencing, yet I thought it odd that I knew nothing of the woman she was.

Mother was 64 years old when she died. I was 40, and I did not know her as a person. At the time, I had no feelings regarding her passing other than believing her suffering was finally over. In fact, I was rather beige to it all when a sheriff from Florida contacted me to tell me of her passing. She was "homeless and indigent," as he put it. I learned from him she had frequented a women's homeless shelter over the years, and this is where she was found deceased.

He offered no comfort and was merely performing his required duty by seeking a place to send her cremains. I was able to later contact the shelter Mother had found as a safe place and discovered she had left behind a few belongings, including an address book through which her siblings were contacted. One of them informed the sheriff how to locate me.

Upon contacting the shelter, the staff informed me she was no longer smoking and that they knew her to be a kind and thoughtful woman who expressed gratitude for their assistance. They never knew my mother had children despite her coming there intermittently for over a decade. It was as if we did not exist for her either. This inexplicably saddened me. Did she forget us secondary to her mental health challenges, or had she chosen not to speak of us for other reasons? Perhaps her heart was broken too? I will never know.

It wasn't until I received my mother's cremains that the reality of it all set in. She, my mother, was dead. It did not register as a typical death that someone of that magnitude should. I did not mourn the loss of her physical presence because I did not know her that way. For months following her death, something was heavy within me. There would be no more chances for reconciliation. No opportunities for change and connection. I would never hear I'm sorry. I would never have a mother. I anguished over this for months and ultimately concluded that hope dies hardest. Without hope, there is nothing to look forward to and nothing to keep me moving forward, or at least treading water for the last ounce of survival. I mourned the loss of hope harder than I had ever mourned losing the woman who was my mother.

Eventually, guilt set in. I had not looked for her, and I had never attempted to intervene or help in any way, except when she made herself available to me by seeking me as a young adult. In fact, as I got older, I had once instructed some of my mother's siblings to refrain from telling her of my whereabouts and that I had children, fearing she would take them as she had told me she would so many years before. I had become the one who was harsh, critical, and unyielding.

Rather than be a victim of my circumstances, I spent a significant amount of time processing my choices and coming to terms with the decisions I had made regarding my mother. It was no easy reckoning, and I was utterly gutted. Working through things revealed many truths, and I now know my mother was my greatest teacher in life, my greatest lesson, and the greatest love there is.

"Step into the fire of self-discovery.
This fire will not burn you;
it will only burn what you are not."

—Mooji

Gifts of Spirit

Parallel to the tumultuous events of childhood was my budding awareness of Self—not the physical me but rather the energetic being inhabiting my body. Along with it came a Knowingness that became increasingly harder to ignore. Both worlds collided, and what was my normal became increasingly dissonant.

As a child, the conversations with spirit were frequent and uplifting. They were my sole source of serenity for years. Despite the impact of our communications, I could not help but feel guilty for not openly acknowledging my spirit friends. I made several attempts to bring this information forward through the everyday occurrences I experienced, such as knowing when the telephone was going to ring and who was calling, even if they had never called our house before, foreseeing the deaths of my maternal grandfather and favorite aunt, and offering people insights and verbal support in the form of messages from loved ones who had passed.

It all seemed relatively innocent from my perspective. I was trying to be helpful. I knew things I should not and could not know for my age and reach, and I often perceived future events; I frequently saw spirit in the form of shimmers of light and experienced a shadow man. I heard music in relation to people and situations when none was playing in the world outside and around me, and I felt other's energy as profoundly as I experienced my own. I experienced the energy of trees, my favorites being maples, willows, and aspens, and I felt a kinship to animals that was, at the time, unexplainable.

The things I experienced were not spoken about by anyone I had ever been exposed to—not in church or other social circles, school or amongst my peers, or my family of origin. The things I experienced were, for all that I knew at the time, associated with mental illness, and I most certainly did not want to be associated with any of that! If my mother's diagnoses and behaviors taught me anything, it was that hearing voices and seeing things others did not see was unacceptable.

I endeavored once to speak with the pastor of our church, having been encouraged by my spirit friends. I was seven years old when I revealed some of my truths to him, only to be told that I was a liar and attention-seeking. I was told my behavior was blasphemous for attempting to present myself as the equivalent of a Saint or Seer, as known in the Holy Bible. While I was doing no such thing, I ultimately learned that religious settings were also not a safe place to reveal my true self nor a place to find acceptance. This encounter changed my relationship with the church so much that it endures today.

I have since forgiven that incident and those involved, and I have overcome its impact to a great degree. One boundary I set to preserve my energetic space was to intentionally distance myself from organized religion. I became aligned with energy and what is now known as spiritual or metaphysical practices. I began to rely on my instincts regarding people and events and quickly learned energy does not lie. Living in this manner was a better fit for my lived experience and it aligned with my personal truths at the time and still does.

While the pastor-related incident taught me to secret the spiritual gifts I was born with, it also taught me to listen to the small voice within, and for that, I am grateful. I continued self-soothing by engaging in communications with spirit, whom at the time I referred to as invisible friends. They were then, and still are today, a source of support and strength on which I rely. I implicitly trust their guidance and endeavor to heed the information they provide.

It wasn't always this way, though. For years, I denounced spiritual experiences despite knowing it as Truth. The journey has been multifaceted, and along the way, I have acquired many blessings. I learned forgiveness and to shine my light, no matter what darkness presents before me. The light of Truth overshadows darkness, for there cannot be darkness without light. This much I know is true.

I believe everything happened as it was intended; otherwise, it would have been different. I am not referring to some predestined plan for my existence, but rather a belief in a methodology to things as they unfold for my enlightenment and development of awareness of Self in form. Of course, this reality was born from everything I endured up to the point of its discovery.

I spent the better part of my childhood conflicted between my reality and what others could believe. Not unlike other empaths, I felt alone and completely misunderstood. I often spoke about not being from here and wanting to go home, which to me at the time was an unknown place in the stars—someplace far, far from Earth and the confines of being human.

I borrowed astronomy books from the library, searching for some semblance of familiarity and secretly hoping to discover my true home. I incurred many library fines for overdue books that begat numerous lectures from my father about respecting the library's property and the value of a dollar. Sadly, I never discovered my true origin.

Rather than spurn other's support and curiosities for my revelations, they drew criticism and almost ineffable condemnation. The final blow came after being verbally admonished by my father to the degree I asked spirit to stop everything, and for the most part, it did.

Oddly enough, the woman father dated and later married was a known psychic and medium to whom he had revealed that his own father and mother were spiritually gifted. I never connected how these experiences were okay for her and yet not okay for me.

Although I no longer perceived big events about to occur and did not hear music or names around people, I continued to feel spirit with me and found their presence immensely comforting. I trusted that my request to cease communication was in my best interest at the time, and I attempted to move forward without them.

Despite my attempts to shut everything off completely, I continued to experience prophetic dreams and deeply intense connections to the Earth and her creatures, and I felt led by a source of wisdom much greater than any human could provide. I had random spiritual experiences related to my maternal grandmother in my late twenties, and I continued to know things I should not. I trusted my sense of things, and while I was not completely in tune with spirit, I was not without them. Later, things stirred more profoundly during my first pregnancy and came fully into being through my first son, who also saw spirit as a very young child.

It wasn't until the passing of my father that I began experiencing spirit again the way I had as a child. The reinitiating event came in the form of a visitation two months after his death, an experience that is as vivid today as it was the Saturday afternoon it occurred. I often reflect on those moments we spent together telepathically communicating and enjoying the impressions of the setting in which it occurred. I find great comfort in knowing he has always been with me.

In the week before his death, my father had been released from the hospital on hospice. I was not allowed to come to his wife's home or to see him since his release almost one week prior. His wife made it very clear that we, my brother and I, were not welcome to visit or call. This was to be her family's exclusive time with our father. She, her parents, her children, and the grandchildren had gathered to be near him for the last few days he was in form.

A week passed, and I had not been informed of anything regarding my father. When I finally called the day before he passed, my step-grandmother answered the phone and questioned intently why I had not come to be with him. When I told her it was under her daughter's direction, the woman gasped and voiced a belief that I was mistaken or there had been some terrible miscommunication. She handed the phone off to my step-grandfather, who made small talk while she made inquiries of my stepsibling regarding the truth of my report.

Discovering some version of this had been told to them, she then confronted my stepmother. I heard the conversation as it occurred loudly in the background. Thankfully, my step-grandmother was having none of it, and my stepmother reluctantly agreed to allow me to come to the house the next afternoon, but only between 5:00 and 5:30 p.m.—no sooner and no later. That was my allotted time with my father. That was it!

I hurriedly planned for my children's care that afternoon, then traveled to my father's house, where my brother was staying, to get him. That afternoon, I arrived with my brother, as instructed, a few minutes before 5:00 p.m. We waited in his truck, feeling oddly out of place, sitting in front of her house until the allotted time. At precisely 5:00, we approached and were greeted at the door by my stepbrother and his wife. My eldest stepsister entered next, and then the youngest. The step-grandparents made an appearance and attempted small talk, all while I moved ever closer to my father as he lay in a hospital bed in the front room. He was awake and coherent, and his frail form appeared almost too weak to exist. I wept inside at the sight of him. It was as if he was almost not even there energetically. It's hard to explain, but if you have ever experienced this, you will know what I mean.

I was not allowed time alone with my father, so one of the related steps was instructed to always be in the room to "monitor the situation." Out of the 30 minutes I was given, they and my brother took up most of my allocated time. In total, the conversation was benign and light, avoidant of anything to do with death and goodbyes. I'm not certain which of us was actively avoiding the subject; everything felt foreign, contrived, and uneasy. I could not speak freely as I was being watched and our conversation scrutinized.

Father asked about the boys, whom I now wished I had brought with me. He deserved to see them one last time, but I couldn't bear what I imagined would be the state of things, and to manage a baby and a two-year-old would have been too much. Even now, pangs of guilt run through me as I write this nearly 18 years later.

The finality of it all came when Father asked us, my brother and I, to take care of each other and to promise to be there for each other always, which we dutifully did. Now was not the time to split hairs and disrespect his request. Father knew my brother and I did not share any closeness and likely knew too that his request would not be carried out.

I gave him one last hug and walked to the door. Before leaving, I turned and saw a frail shadow of a man seated on the side of the bed as he readied to take more pain medication. I said, "I love you, Daddy," to which he responded, "I love you too, Boo." This was the last time I ever saw my father in form.

My mind was numb with grief. I don't remember the drive back to my father's house or the conversation that ensued with my brother, other than being told I was to get nothing of my father's after he passed. Not even a block away from my stepmother's house, my brother spelled out very clearly that nothing of our fathers would be mine.

At the time, it did not register. It did not matter. My father was dying. My heart ached for all that was lost and could never be. The drive home was arduous; my mind raced and was blank at the same time. After returning home, I sat with the children and went through the nighttime routine as if on autopilot. I knew my father's end was near, and I dreaded going to sleep that night. Somehow, I knew that when I awoke I would not have a father.

It was a hard-won battle to fall asleep only to have a premonition of Father's death. I dreamed of delivering his eulogy, speaking as tears welled from deep within and streamed from my eyes. My chest was tight with anguish as I tried to relay to those who had gathered what a loving man my father was, how different our lives would be without him, and how deeply he would be missed. I do not recall much from the prose I spoke, save for one passage, "For those of us who were blessed to know him, my dad left footprints on our hearts." I was awoken from this dream by my then-husband to be told my father had passed.

In the early morning hours, my father slipped silently from physical presence. He had graduated from this Earthly existence following a 10-year relationship with two forms of cancer. All he was meant to experience was accomplished. Lives he was meant to touch, experiences and lessons, moments created and shared. In one final exhalation, his journey was complete—only to begin anew at that exact moment.

On the day of his funeral, I stood before the congregation of his wife's church, holding my infant son, and delivered the words I had dreamt on the night of his passing. Following the church service, we proceeded to the cemetery just outside town, where many were honored to experience him one last time.

As the procession came to rest in a small cemetery in northern Minnesota, many of us noticed an American bald eagle perched in an oddly huge, gnarled, and mostly dead maple tree. Those who knew my father well noted its presence and marveled that today, of all days, this experience occurred, the American bald eagle being my father's favorite bird and the sugar maple his favorite tree. He was there, with us, as we laid his human form in its final resting place. Many took comfort in his presence that day.

In the years preceding his physical death, multiple factors came between us and the closeness we once shared as father and daughter when I was a small child. None of that mattered now; in fact, it had begun to matter less and less as years lapsed before the dawning of this day.

As I grew and experienced life, emotional maturity and logical reasoning offered refuge and solace. I sought comfort within my human mind analyzing, defining, quantifying, and qualifying our interactions based on arbitrary snippets that comprised our lives together, immeasurable in every way other than the value I assigned and the emotions woven of the threads of thought. Still, it was what I had created and clung to and my way of making sense of it all. This allowed me to accept things as they were, for what they were. Nothing more. Nothing less. It was what it was. Empty. Hollow. Abandoned.

In the days and weeks following Father's death, many events began to surface, aligning in an idiosyncratic yet plausible manner. I began to experience my existence, purpose, and being far beyond the human experience. The awakening surpassed any knowledge I previously held through scholarly means. My awareness of life, my primary life force, felt unfamiliar and comfortable at the same time. I accepted unquestionably that it all lay dormant within me, waiting for this very moment. Feeling like I was coming home to myself, I became increasingly excited about the journey ahead.

The Visitation

A mere two months after my father's passing, I was gifted an experience of undoubtable existence beyond the physical world and the human experience I knew as life. The visitation from my father was unexplainable in any other terms than extraordinary. If I were any kind of artist, I would have captured every detail while it was still fresh in my mind for fear it would fade with time. Now, 18 years later, I remember the details as vividly as the day it occurred. Forever impressed upon my physical mind, I know the energetic impression of the experience is eternal.

The spiritual visitation was like a waking dream, yet not a dream. I was completely aware of my surroundings, the happenings and goings on around me, all the while being aware of an energetic connection playing out in my mind's eye. A state of being similar to extreme relaxation and lightly veiled awareness, similar to that which you experience when beginning to fall asleep or immediately upon beginning to wake. A visitation is not a dream; it is an energetic connection, most often with someone no longer in physical form.

It was a Saturday afternoon in July, and I had just gotten both boys down for a nap. I lay down, hoping for a few moments of rest, and I was comforted hearing the children breathing rhythmically through the baby monitor on the nightstand beside me.

Not long after lying on my bed, I drifted between wakefulness and sleep, aware of the sounds and environment around me, yet surrounded by another plane of existence. I slid effortlessly into the universal abyss before me. After a few minutes in this space, I felt someone lay beside me. And so it began, a life-altering encounter with love as it can only be known by the soul. A journey of complete acceptance, forgiveness, reconciliation, and closure.

The impressions began with driving a familiar road as my brother and I sought fervently for signs. Urged ever forward, we were certain to discover what we sought if only we would drive a little further. Fraught with angst and racing the pending darkness, we pushed on along a long and lonely highway through the Canadian wilderness of Ontario, one we traveled frequently in happier times.

This day was different, and we both subconsciously knew the cost. We were in search of a rustic log cabin on the edge of a lake; its entrance was graced with three sizable stone fountains. Every side road brought uncontainable excitement and inevitable disillusionment when nothing we searched for was revealed. We were running out of time and roads.

Nearing the end of what, in my imagination, was to be the Manitou Road, a desolate connection point between Fort Francis and Dryden, Ontario, and fearing daylight would usurp us, we decided to turn back. Sullen and bereft, we slowed and veered to the right. We turned onto a sloping road and then stopped short. Dumbfounded, there before us was the cabin and, to its right, three stone fountains. Excitement overwhelmed us as we enthusiastically parked the old truck and jumped from its uncomfortable seats. The trip had been a long one thus far. We stretched and yawned generously before making our way toward the door.

As we approached the cabin, the splashing fountains beckoned me to look in their direction. Doing so, I noted several boats docked a few yards away. I marveled that, somehow, it was now just shortly after sunrise. The sun's golden glow, still low in the sky, glimmered and danced across the water as steam rose from the vast, liquescent space lined with trees. Turning back toward the cabin, it too had changed and now resembled a great log lodge.

We proceeded up the stairs, across the grand deck, and pulled open the heavy wooden door. Once inside, we were greeted by a familiar voice. I looked around, focusing now on a glass display case that held candy and trinkets, adorned with a cash register and a tin tray of peppermint candies. A welcome surprise. The figure behind the case came slowly into focus as I heard, "What can I do ya' for?" as the individual turned our direction. To my surprise, my aunt, 20 years passed, laughingly exclaimed, "Well, look what the cat dragged in!" Greeting us with a warm welcome, she said it was good to see us again and boldly stated, "I know who you're here to see!" She quickly turned on her heel and led us across a large room with vaulted ceilings, great log beams, a grand stone fireplace, and a wall of windows that opened into the vast Canadian wilderness.

Busy surveying the room, taking it all in, I was too distracted to notice where we were going. The room was afire with the glow of the morning sun; people-filled booths lined the edges of the room, and others sat scattered at tables throughout the space. The smells wafting through the air were succulent. An inaudible din of conversation in the background set the tone and energy of the room. Suddenly, we stopped, my aunt moved aside, and sitting at a small table was a petite and frail man in a familiar flannel shirt, donning an even more familiar cap.

My father stood to welcome us with a wide toothy grin and a big hug, as he always had. Genuinely happy to see us, he exuded joy. It was literally radiating from him like a warm-toned glow. He motioned for us to sit and greeted a passing waitress for some assistance when she had a moment, of course. Polite and patient, that was my dad. He sat with his back to the great wall of windows, with a space between our table and the row of booths behind us where waitresses moved about from table to table as groups of patrons came and went. When the waitress came to the table, he joyfully boasted about us, his children, as he made introductions. We ordered and things fell into a comfortable flow.

Father began by asking how the drive was and made small talk, detailing numerous accounts of our travels together along the same road so many years ago, even as it was being built in the late 1970s. As we shared, becoming more focused on our conversation, the rest of the room (including my brother) faded into the background. Soon, it was just Dad and me. Talking, laughing, reminiscing, and crying together in that magical space. It felt so good to see him! I was giddy and unable to focus completely at first. All I knew was how good it felt to be near him once again, to hear his voice, and to have an opportunity to catch up. Things felt different. The energy had changed for the better, and I enjoyed it.

I remember thinking, "This can't be real; he's dead," but it was very real. I couldn't make up the conversations we were having. Not in a million years! He carefully and thoughtfully attended to every detail, question, and emotion raised within me as we reviewed our lives together. He was understanding in a way I had not known him to be previously.

Attentively, compassionately, and lovingly, he led me to places within me that I never knew existed. He helped me view our life circumstances from a different perspective, one of love without conditions and complete acceptance in a space void of judgment. Nothing was labeled or defined; it just was.

I could understand each detail from the human perspective, his and mine, and from a very different place outside of my existence in form. A space that allowed each interaction to be a vital lesson for the energy within me that made my human condition such that it is. The event was so surreal and profound that at times, even now, I explore the depths of those moments, hoping to glean even more than I had initially. My human was and is in awe of it all.

As suddenly as it began, it was over. My brother appeared as if from thin air. He said it was time to leave, briefly detailing the long drive ahead. Knowing he was right, Dad and I pushed our chairs back from the table and arose in unison, exchanging pleasantries about how nice it was to see each other again and how thankful we were for this time together.

I said, "I love you, Daddy. I miss you so much. There is so much I want to share with you." He responded, "I love you too, Boo," his nickname for me since I was a little girl. I stepped toward him as he opened his arms.

As we hugged, I suddenly became aware that he was transparent. Rocking back on my heels, I said, "Daddy, I don't understand. What's happening?" My father replied, "You will have to hug me a little harder; I can't feel everything the same way from where I am now." In that moment, the entire day played out in my mind's eye as I stood before him. A fast-forward version of the comings and goings, our conversations, and the sunlight as it danced across the room, casting shadows as the end of the day neared.

One thing stood out that I had not noticed. As the day played out before me, I saw everything through my father's image. Sunlight glinted on particles as they floated in the air, passing through him. Rays of golden joy spread across the room; they shone through him in a luminous radiance, unlike anything I had ever seen. He smiled and nodded, a knowing nod, acknowledging my new truth. He said, "Know that I am proud of you, who you have become, and who you will continue to be. There is no end. We continue. I am always with you."

I became more aware of my surroundings as the veil between spirit and physical presence thinned. I smelled my father all around me and began to weep. I wept for the ache, deep within me, to have him here in the physical world. I wept for the ending of our time together in spirit. I wept, too, for the depth of his presence and the love I had experienced.

Immediately following the visitation, life began to change. I felt energetically lighter, more deeply attuned to those around me, and somehow expansive beyond my physical body. The remainder of the day appeared somehow more vivid; my children's energy felt vibrant and harmonious, and I experienced a unity within me that has since been unparalleled.

The night of the visitation, I welcomed the opportunity for more experiences with spirit and excitedly awaited bedtime. Sleep came effortlessly and was deeper than it had been for weeks. My slumber was broken twice to feed the baby and then again at precisely 3:11 a.m. when I awoke compelled by an urgency to connect with spirit. Oddly wide awake, I did not hesitate to get out of bed. I was anxious to begin writing and see what would come through.

On the initial night of connection, things flowed without hesitancy. I wrote for nearly 90 minutes before spirit indicated it was time to get on with the rest of the day. Believing it had been a one-off occurrence, I was pleasantly surprised the communications continued nightly at precisely 3:11 a.m.

I awoke feeling rested and excited to meet with spirit every night for several weeks. Through our sessions together, I learned to connect more fully with my higher self and the physical form I inhabit. Those few weeks of early morning blending with spirit spurned my curiosity and fed my incessant inquisitiveness.

Urged by my spirit team, I began researching spiritual associations with 3:11, which led to my discovery of Sikhism and the Sanskrit language. One area led effortlessly to the next, each building solidly upon the other. The lessons continued, as did my exploration of numerous other areas. Topics I had not previously thought were interesting suddenly became intriguing, and I voraciously devoured information.

I studied concepts related to astronomy, tarot, and numerology; topics related to Western medicine, Tai Chi and Qigong, Reiki, and Buddhism; became involved in the practices of meditation, breathwork, and yoga; studied psychism, channeling, and mediumship; and became proficient in performing hypnosis and parallel/past-life regression. I felt responsible for supporting my soul's evolution through the rediscovery of Self in form, and my mind was like a sponge absorbing everything I could to self-educate. Thankfully, I was also gifted with a thirst for knowledge for the sake of knowing, which has served me well since childhood.

In the years since the visitation, I have continued to experience the presence of my father's energy. The gifts of soul shared that day allowed me to heal in the physical world and offered me access to the universe for my soul to explore. For that, I am eternally grateful.

Admittedly, I have since pondered my brother's presence in the experience with my father. I was told shortly after my father's passing that my brother had words with our father in the days preceding his death, during which he detailed his thoughts and feelings about many events that transpired central to my father's relationship with his then-wife.

In doing so, he related that he had always had my dad, even after our mother was gone, and made his perception very clear that I had no one and was abandoned by them both. I reacted strongly to this information initially, even though I realized my brother had a right to express himself as he did. I believed it was the incorrect time, as father was dying, yet I knew it had to be said for everyone's sake. We all seek closure in our own way—not rightly or wrongly, just differently.

Regarding my brother's presence in the visitation experience, I have allowed the meaning to reveal itself to me and have come to know my truth. I believe my brother's soul led me to Father. They were close in physical life, which has carried over into the nonphysical realm. My brother was my guide. For that, too, I am grateful.

Since the time of my father's passing and the visitation, spirit has repeatedly revealed to me in profound and undeniably impactful ways. I have been shown star systems beyond the known reality of our solar system and journeyed via astral projections that allowed me to be close to those I love in their time of distress and even while dying. I have been blessed to communicate with individuals no longer in form and entities who have never been human. Telepathic communications, the psychic knowingness of an individual's energy, and being a channel for spirit are my all-time favorite gifts thus far!

Unexpected Insights

Blessings come when we least expect them, and if we are open to receiving them, one's perspective can be changed. Approximately four years after my father's passing, a tragic near accident revealed to me a guardian angel. While at the time I was not so certain I still believed in angels, there was no denying the presence of mine when my vehicle was sliding on an icy road and unable to stop. Then it suddenly moved to the right in a 90-degree manner, turning completely parallel to the road I was approaching at 40 miles per hour with my two small children nestled in their carriers in the back seat, completely unaware of what was happening, as my car came to a gentle stop just in time to avoid collision with a double-bladed snowplow heading directly at us at a high rate of speed. The final resting place of my car allowed room for the plow driver to maneuver past us without so much as a scrape! Admittedly, I was aghast and afraid for my children. Had there been an impact, my four-year-old and I would have certainly perished had we been hit broadside.

After the plow passed, I took a minute to gather my thoughts before continuing about the day's tasks, which included driving some 15 miles to bring the children to day-care and school and myself to work. The boys did not appear to notice anything unusual other than we were now going in the wrong direction. They sat safely snuggled in their car seats and marveled at the snowplow and how big it was. They were both in a developmental stage of being fascinated with big construction equipment, and this one was humongous!

After delivering the children, I hesitantly got back in my vehicle, intent on traveling across town to work. Attempting to convince myself I needed the distraction, what I wanted to do was gather the boys and go home for a day of snuggles and love, but work was looming. My mind was completely blank, which was not my norm. I usually had nothing short of what seemed to be several hundred thoughts running through it every minute I was awake. Right now, at that moment, nothing.

Something was amiss. I could not put my finger on it; I just knew I could not be at work that day, especially not after what we just experienced. I am not an alarmist, and to be honest, I don't recall feeling any particular way about what had happened. To the best of my recollection, I was not shaken up, weepy, or otherwise off mentally or physically. I just knew, with every ounce of my being, I needed to go home.

With next to no consideration for my workload, coworkers, or the impending things I was required to address that day, I "banged in," federal prison slang for calling in sick. I immediately felt guilty because taking a sick day was not something I did, especially not to address my own mental or physical health.

With the deed done, I turned toward home, feeling pulled in that direction. At the edge of the small town where I worked, a sense of serenity came over me that felt like a profound, energetic shift had occurred. I was completely calm, with no thought in my head, yet I was acutely aware of my surroundings.

Closer to my hometown, I approached a cornfield with a unique tree on a hill I had long admired. As I got closer, I heard a soft voice say, "Do you see me?" For a split second, I thought I was experiencing some residual trauma from the near miss earlier that morning or that perhaps I had forgotten one of the boys in the back seat of the car. I looked in the mirror. No children. I continued driving.

The voice appeared again, excited and almost childlike, and said again, "Do you see me? Over here!" I felt an overwhelming urge to stop the car, which I did. Dumbfounded, I exited the car, thinking surely it was something in the automobile. I then heard, "Over here. Look! Do you see me now?" I looked toward the tree in the field, and beside it was a brilliant, bright white light with a glowing bluish outline.

When I saw it, I gasped audibly. I fumbled for my cell phone, almost unable to believe what I was seeing, but somehow knowing I needed to document this moment. First, I looked through the phone's camera and then without. Whatever it was, the glowing brightness was still there. I took a quick picture, not certain it would even appear in the image.

The communication continued. "It's okay. It's all going to be okay." I burst into tears as I dropped to my knees. The voice said again, "It's okay. You're okay." I heard myself uttering "thank you," as I gathered my composure enough to take several more photos as the light rose from the side of the tree before vanishing slightly above it. I sat on the ground for a few moments as vehicles whizzed by, when something within me suddenly became aware I was sitting on the side of a very busy county road—a completely unsafe situation.

I slowly stood, gazed at the tree for a moment, and then continued the drive home in what I can only describe as utter disbelief. Once home, I detailed the entire experience in my journal and marveled several times at the images of what I now believed to be my guardian angel, feeling infinitely blessed I was able to capture the moment in an indelible image. The rest of the day is a complete blur. For a matter-of-fact person who is a no-nonsense gal, I realized I had experienced something unexplainable in terms of things I had, to that point, experienced—something ethereal and not of this world.

Revelations

The magic continued when, a year or so later, I experienced a visitation from my mother. Shocked and surprised at the time, I now see how it all fits together. Mother came through during a metaphysical workshop while I was performing a soul-gazing exercise with a woman I just met. The exercise involved sitting while facing an individual and looking into their eyes without averting one's gaze—no easy feat for someone who does not like to be seen!

I was feeling increasingly uncomfortable and experiencing an insurmountable urge to look away when, suddenly, the woman's face morphed into that of my mother. While we were to be silent, somewhere within me, a voice came, and I blurted out, "Why didn't you love me?" The woman responded in kind, without missing a beat, "It was because I loved you the most." We were both surprised by these utterances and the facilitator, noticing our noncompliance with the instructions and likely fearing we would disrupt others in the group, approached to ascertain the situation. In revealing what transpired, she then took several moments to help us process the occurrence, such that we could in a room full of people.

Admittedly, my mother's words set me back and did not resonate fully. In fact, everything within my cognitive and emotional being refuted the words. *Loved me*, I thought. You didn't know what love was, in my honest opinion, let alone how to show me love.

I became angry, of course, as the first step of self-preservation. Doing so allowed me to push away the ever-present pain I now felt. Years of hurt, fear, rejection, and sadness occurred all at once, uncontained and unrestrained, threatening to take over my very being in a room full of strangers. I was not ready to process my feelings and was not interested in what this event meant.

As a secondary emotion, the anger partly hid my increasing discomfort, disbelief, and dissonance that welled from deep within. Her revelation shook me to the core. Not to mention how a frail, elderly, and unassuming grey-haired woman could present as a robust, much younger, curly-haired redhead had my ego mind spinning to make sense of it all.

Unable to avoid the incessant urgings of spirit, I later explored my mother's visitation and was sent down a new path—a journey of opening my heart, receiving energetic attunements, and release. Throughout my time processing it all, my mother's presence was prominent in each moment, and I felt blessed to know she was with me now in a way she could not be while in form.

Everything culminated in my mother speaking to me and eventually channeling a letter through me explaining her soul's position regarding our physical time together. This contact with her offered an unexpected sense of peace and closure I did not know I needed.

Later that same year, my experiences with my mother were unequivocally confirmed by a source outside myself when I attended an event hosted by an internationally known medium, just as I had several times in the past.

Having never been read by him, I did not expect that night to be any different, and I could not have been more wrong! Not only did he provide messages of love, confirmation of her presence, and knowledge of my life's events, he also told me of the words my mother channeled through me in the letter I had written on Mother's Day that same year. Several signs from my mother presented repeatedly in the following days and weeks.

The experience of freedom I have known since that night is unparalleled. Unburdened and now thankful for our time together, I am aware of the many gifts my mother presented and shared throughout my lived experience and my connection with her after her departure in the physical. I now know she conspired to present opportunities for me to grow by initiating many experiences meant to challenge and enhance my undertakings of awakening to the Reality of my existence.

For that, I am eternally grateful. What deeper love is there than to volunteer and perform as the catalyst for another's lived experience—the impact from which an individual must navigate to arrive at self?

Arriving at Wholeness

I see, hear, and feel spirit every day and honor their desire to communicate with and through me. As a receiver of spirit, I feel humbled by their willingness to impart knowledge. Blessed to study mediumship with some of the world's foremost mentors, I continued energy work for several years, became proficient in conducting parallel/past-life regressions and hypnotherapy focused on one's communication with the higher self and universal consciousness. I also studied various energy healing modalities, none of which I am proficient enough to provide for others' benefit. I have experienced countless contacts and occurrences—each uniquely astounding, yet with a comforting familiarity.

I experienced energetic healing from an entity who works through a world-renowned medium and channel. This experience changed my perspective of self and the form I inhabit (my human) and healed a neck and spine injury caused by a rear-end traffic collision. It was nothing short of miraculous! Although it was several years ago, this experience feels like it occurred yesterday. And, in a way—at least energetically speaking—it did.

My curiosity abounds, as does my pursuit of knowledge of the spirit world. Although my spiritual gifts have changed over time, I endeavor to remain open to whatever is presented. I now see the energy of plants and trees, which is relatively new. Rather than feeling auras and intuitively sensing their colors, I am becoming capable of visualizing them in their fullness.

For years, I felt compelled and responsible to pursue every energetic gift I received. To that end, I spent several years bouncing from one modality to another, like a crow collecting shiny things, yet never becoming fully adept at any one thing. Everything was interesting, and nothing seemed impossible or out of reach. I was like a kid in a candy store with nothing off-limits!

Over the years, I became increasingly frustrated with not becoming proficient in any modality. A perfectionist at heart, I decided to dial in on a few areas of particular interest where things flowed more naturally. Thus began my fervent drive to understand energy at its very basis of being.

From there, everything else fell perfectly into place. I trusted spirit to lead me exactly where I was meant to go, and I am thankful for their gentle and not-so-gentle nudges along the way. The happy detours and side trips presented many lessons that ultimately became the path.

Journey to Source

The story of my beginnings and the journey to self thus far would not be complete without mention of my first regression experience.

A regression is the facilitation of a hypnotic state wherein the participant is led to have the experience or at least the impression of a former incarnation. Generally undertaken to assist the individual in revealing any expressions in this life brought forward to be resolved, the hypnotic state of regression is believed to access information that cannot otherwise be achieved in a waking, conscious state. Some believe all lives occur concurrently in a parallel reality to the current lived experience rather than a previous life being accessed. That said, I encourage those interested to explore their individual truths related to such matters.

Though I was all in for the regression experience and with not an ounce of skepticism, it was difficult to get out of my head. Type-A, as I wanted to be and used to managing the narrative, I could not shut my mental narrative off enough to surrender completely to the experience.

If it was going to happen, I wanted to remember every thought and sensation from when it began. My overzealousness only served to impede the process. I lay there entirely too long, worried the individual conducting the regression would end the experience. I argued, cajoled, and berated myself in my head to encourage the process, to no avail. I had all but given up when something shifted, and I immediately abandoned my attempts to manipulate its outcome. Surrender, at last! When that occurred, everything changed.

The regression was led as part of a weekend workshop focused on teaching introductory principles and practice techniques of psychic development. People from all walks of life gathered to share their skills and abilities, each with special and unique gifts and perspectives and each with different levels of awareness and understanding. It was a good group to learn from and with.

At the onset of the initial session, the course outline was distributed along with other materials. I was thrilled and apprehensive at the same time to learn regression was a part of this offering. I had read the works of prominent authors in this field and had been fascinated with the concept of regression for several years. As one who has a history of experiencing technical difficulties with any visualization exercise, my anxiety began to rise. Knowing the best way for me to decrease anxiety is to become familiar with the challenge, I used the time between activities and away from class to familiarize myself with concepts related to regression specific to being an actual participant. In doing so, I grew increasingly skeptical of my ability to have a genuine experience.

The last day of the workshop arrived, and the time was now upon me. Along with everyone else, I chose a place on the floor and made myself as comfortable as possible while excitedly hoping for the best. Exceedingly detailed and specific instructions were provided. Participants were requested to review the overarching theme of this incarnation and, during the regression, go back to a time in a former life when we felt as we primarily had in our present lifetime.

Upon hearing the directions, I became acutely aware that I did not belong here. Not here in this room or in this place in time. This felt immensely right, as if I was on the verge of some great discovery. As for my incarnation, the impression I received at a soul level was that I was not from here, at least not originally. A brief review of my life thus far concluded I have always felt as though I do not belong on Earth and certainly not in human form. My physical body never seemed to fit well.

As the facilitator continued to answer questions and provide reassurance to other participants, I fondly remembered all the astronomy books I borrowed from the local library as a young child, often keeping them long after the due date despite incurring fines my father had to pay and the lectures about the fines I had to endure. I willingly accepted his perspectives about responsibility and the value of a dollar. It was a fair trade for a few more days with my precious books. They were my direct link of escape into the stars.

The faint sound of a bell ended my daydream, and my awareness shifted focus to the here and now. The regression was beginning. After a brief grounding and centering exercise, we began to relax on the floor as sounds around us faded. At first, and for what seemed like forever, I could not let go to the level required. It's no surprise my ego mind's innate desire to maintain control managed to creep into even this setting.

Convinced I would not have a regression experience, I settled mentally and physically, relaxing into the space. The facilitator's voice became an extraneous background vibration that ebbed and flowed like shallow waves on a beach. Feeling as though I was falling asleep or, at the very least, losing awareness of the sensations associated with my current surroundings, it was then that it began.

Somewhere on a level of consciousness between awake and asleep, I found myself experiencing vivid impressions playing out like two old film reels running parallel in the spaces on either side of me. I was now in this newly created space, not a physical body but rather an impression of myself. The backdrop was a vast star field that appeared endless. I felt as though I was walking amongst millions and millions of stars. Yet, there was nothing to support me, no path or trail to follow. Seemingly limitless in all directions, I saw stars everywhere—above, below, and around me. I suddenly felt chilled and did not want to reach for my blanket, fearing the experience would end.

The infinite darkness impressed upon me that I was no longer on Earth, and my soul had journeyed far beyond the physical form it inhabited. Like independent movie reels playing simultaneously on the outermost perimeter of my mind's peripheral vision, I became aware the films had individual frames, and within these frames were scenes that played out within each of them. I glimpsed bits and pieces as they moved by.

At first, the reels moved slowly, playing various out-of-focus scenes. Attempts to focus on one frame or slow them from passing were futile. Gradually, frame by frame, they began to move faster, and the images became more focused. I was able to identify moments as if they were still occurring in a time parallel to my present reality. Perceiving that what I was searching for was not within this experience, I heeded the sense of urgency to journey beyond this point. That's when things became interesting.

The facilitator's voice was faint in the background and sounded far, far away. Frames continued moving by, or rather, the awareness now became that I was moving past them. It appeared my thoughts or awareness controlled the speed at which things progressed. With this awareness, the rate at which I moved became increasingly swift, so much so that the films disappeared completely.

I found myself in a vast area of complete darkness with nothing above or below me, in front or behind me. I was in a limitless dark space. Before I had time to panic, I began drifting toward an immense luminescent tube. Glimmering silvery white with mutable density, it was in constant motion within itself. The tube itself was much like one would imagine the aurora borealis to be. My excitement grew when I would have expected hesitancy; I felt as if I were about to deboard an airplane to find my tribe waiting. Joyous excitement filled me.

Hovering briefly before its opening, I recall straining to take it all in. My mental self attempted to interrupt the process, and I could feel its presence as a sharply unwelcome intrusion. With the self, such that I was positioned as central as possible within the opening, I marveled at how large it was. It appeared enormous at multiple times my human height, yet despite this, was not looming. Reaching out to touch the glimmering substance, I noted it was cooler than the surrounding atmosphere and imparted an energy that was light and dense at the same time. It was unlike anything I had ever felt.

I became aware of moving further into the tube, and my energy changed. As if every molecule of my being was lighter than air, my vibration increased substantially and began to match my surrounding cocoon of light.

Advancing now through the tube, slowly at first and then at great speed, I appeared to be floating as it moved by me, yet I was accelerating. The tube had numerous twists and turns, peaks and valleys, carrying me far away from my known existence. As I traveled, I could see through the veil of light and was impressed with the vastness of the star fields and galaxies before me.

As quickly as it began, my transition ended. The tube ceased to exist as if it had never existed. I peered into the darkness to take in my surroundings. Faced with a limitless yet seemingly familiar cold darkness, I believed myself back where I began. Admittedly, this was an immense letdown. I had feelings associated with a long-awaited homecoming and found nothing in its place.

Pondering briefly how incredible the experience was, I became aware of an immeasurable shimmering silvery-blue light in the distance. It was as if I saw a metropolitan area glowing on the horizon. I became excited, gleeful, and almost giddy at the sight. As it moved steadily closer, the light grew in intensity. I became overwhelmed with excitement for no apparent reason.

After a moment, I was enveloped in an indescribable light energy. Before me were hundreds, if not thousands, of silvery-blue iridescent energies appearing to loosely mimic human form without distinct features of any kind—no fingers or toes and no genitals or facial features. Approximately four feet in height, they had the most glorious energy and an incredible means of communication—telepathic thought forms.

Suddenly able to communicate telepathically, I received many joyful greetings and an overwhelming sense of belonging, akin to coming home and being missed as if absent for lifetimes. Of the collective gathered there, one entity came forward to communicate. I immediately received the impression of my father's energy. Thought forms exchanged between us at lightning-like speed. Lifetimes of information were relayed in seconds of communication. Impressed upon me were significant events from this incarnation and, better yet, specific individuals who were now in spirit, all of whom had come to greet me. Some stood out more than others, yet all were sending a positive and radiating energy to me.

Instructions from the facilitator played into my awareness, "As you travel backward in time, review the lifetimes you have had. Seek a past life to explore where you experienced the feelings you have had in this one." Rather than focus on any negative connotation, the intent was to connect and gain or regain awareness of what was brought forward into this lifetime.

Again, thought form exchanges of communication ensued between the representative entity before me as it moved ever closer. Now, immediately before me, I recognized a familiarity with this entity, a knowingness and closeness that spanned more than this moment, much more than one human lifetime. Our energetic togetherness was infinite. I was bursting with a sense of intense love and belonging, and I was humbled that the energy chosen to greet me was one I had been with since my origin. I noted a sense of almost palpable safeness and a love beyond measure surrounding me.

The main entity and I communicated back and forth for a short while, and others with whom I had incarnated during this life, now in spirit, also chimed in, doing so in a manner I would recognize, generally with the impression of their once human voice or a familiar telepathic image. Numerous energies came forward in this manner, one after another, presenting with an immeasurable loving presence. I was fascinated by them all, feeling as though we were somehow ultimately one.

Every communication was facilitated through an effortless exchange of energy. As the interactions took place, I became aware that the energies knew my purpose for the regression, and each volunteered to greet me and aid in my soul's experience. The task was twofold: to ease my transition into this space with a familiar and loving being and to serve as one voice for ease of communication, although this was unnecessary. In spirit, we are all one, thus our communication is all known through this universal oneness. It appeared the most familiar energy was the universal communicator of this group, at least in their exchanges with me, which was more for my benefit than anything else.

We agreed my primary objective was to experience, in this space, the theme central to my emotional existence during this life. Completely trusting our universal oneness, the lesson began. The main entity, who I believed to be my father, came forward and blended its energy with mine.

I have no words to describe this experience. The intensity pales by the sheer lack of vividness of words our language affords. I will, however, endeavor to be as descriptive as possible. As the energy surrounded me, I perceived warmth with fullness, creating an unwavering sensation of calm. It permeated my being. The lightness of the energy was surprising, given the immense density with which it enveloped me, feeling like an invisible cloak of sorts.

There was an expansive knowing of our oneness spanning beyond mental comprehension. It instilled within me an awareness of universal consciousness, all being of one, connected and thus all-knowing. Looking back, I would have thought this to create fear, but I was without fear. I learned it is only through love that the understanding of all is created. No judgment or seeking to understand, only knowingness and acceptance of what is as it is and the awareness it is such that it is.

The other energies joined, one by one, until those most familiar to me and I had merged. Completely encircled by them, our energies intermingled, and the collective frequency increased. The remaining beings then surrounded me. I was literally pulsating with energy and glowing as radiant love. In unison, we again raised the frequency of our collective energies. The sensation of completeness, the breadth and depth of love I experienced, filled me through and through as if I would literally burst. Somehow, space for limitless expansion remained. My being had no limitations.

The love energy moved through me, within me, and around me. I radiated love and took it in from the energies surrounding me. I was one with the universe, an infinite and expansive being of love. This was the sensation I yearned for and had been searching for my entire life. At last, I was home! I had achieved oneness with my soul family.

A few moments passed in this blissful state, during which I determined I never wanted to return to form. It became apparent why souls do not possess full awareness of our origin when we incarnate. This was too good, too incredible to be without. Unattainable in human form, the sensations of warmth, fullness, calmness, and undulating waves of love would be too much for any human to experience fully. The expansive frequency alone would short-circuit the physical body's nervous system. In spirit, however, this was the norm. It was then I realized transitioning to spirit was nothing short of miraculous.

The sensation of love in spirit exists at a level unfathomable to those in human form.

The intensity was broken when the main communicator reminded me of our purpose. We again exchanged thought forms, agreeing we must create my human experience, such that I have felt during this incarnation. It was created from love and for contrast and comparison, as was the intent of this regression. I perceived this was one of my soul's many lessons.

In unison, the energy level gradually decreased. As the frequency reduced, the entities began moving away but remained in a circle around me to provide a sense of safety and support. As the entities continued to move further and further away, I was continually reassured that everything would be okay and that this was merely a representation of my Earth-bound experience.

They sensed my apprehension and ensuing sadness. Several entities, those closest to me during this lifetime, remained near yet began separating their energy from mine. Being in their presence and unable to sense the energy created a chasm. The physical proximity was one thing, but the inability to mingle energy left me feeling desperately alone, disconnected, and abandoned. This was an alone unlike anything I had ever experienced, an intensity much greater than that of anything I endured as a human. Yet, it was all too familiar.

I began to sob, reflecting on my soul's experience. It welled from deep within and overtook me. Sobs from a place so primal, I feared what may come next. My body was wracked with an intense emotional pain so great that I wept uncontrollably. With every ounce of my being, I sobbed. For all I never achieved, for all I had lost, and for those who had transitioned to spirit before me. I wept, too, longing to remain with them.

From the depths of me, I experienced the loss of connection and the immense longing of being disconnected. Worse than any loss in my human existence, the intensity of this moment far surpassed anything I could have ever imagined.

After what seemed like an eternity, the frequency stabilized once again, returning to the initial experience. The sensations of warmth, fullness, calmness, and love enveloped me once more with the familiar and welcomed density only their energy could create. The main entity again came forward and comforted me. Many of the entities present reassured me that we had completed our objective and that I had done well with the process. Nothing but radiant love was moving through and around me.

As I became aware of the facilitator counting backward, we exchanged parting communications. I felt a sadness stirring in me as I moved back into this space, now knowing there was so much more. The entire regression spanned approximately 95 minutes yet felt like lifetimes and a split second all at once. I had so many questions. How could it have been possible to experience so much in such a short time? To where did I regress, project, or astral travel? When and where was the origin of my being?

Culminations and Outcomes

While the unknown outweighs the known on an average day, this experience was life-changing. Although many questions were answered, many remained. I gained a better understanding of my soul, who I am within form, and my purpose here. I now implicitly trust the universe will reveal the answers as I am able to comprehend and make the best use of the awareness.

Once fearful of death and of leaving behind those whom I hold dear, I now view transitioning from the physical to pure frequency in a much different way. While I know a part of my human existence is to experience intense emotions for those who will remain after my passing, I also know the time between my transition and theirs is instantaneous in a universal sense. Time, as we experience it physically, does not exist in spirit. I know, too, that when those with whom I have learned and loved in this incarnation pass into spirit, we will all be together again to plan our next grand adventures.

Since my regression experience to Source, I have felt tremendously grateful for my connection with others and my connection with my human. I continue to receive messages from my spirit guides, and I implicitly trust the guidance received. The information is shared with others, as directed, for their messages are not solely mine, but for us all as we share a union one with the other and with the Divine of our creation.

While I now welcome the human journey in its entirety, I am a long way from where my physical life began. Many years, tears, and relationships later, I have learned what love is and, more importantly, what love is not. I learned that to be love, as love was intended to be expressed and ultimately experienced, it must exist without expectation. Love can only exist through acceptance. I also learned that I am the embodiment of love, and to live from a space of love requires consistent conscious effort. I believe this is my purpose in life. I have learned that those with whom we walk the journey are not always those with whom it began. This I have learned to accept as my truth.

As infants, we are more deeply connected to our energetic beings. This ensures, in part, our survival while our intellect and other life skills develop. We intuitively read people's energy and quickly learn to respond in kind. The consequences and rewards of our interactions with the world around us, in essence, shape our behavior. The energy of a harsh environment creates dissonance for the emotionality of a small child, while the soul-self strives to emerge. It is difficult for a child to exist in an environment where love is not the primary language of the words and acts she is exposed to.

Ultimately, we learn to speak the language of our environment at the expense of quelling the voice within. This results in a moving away from the guidance of the spirit and the development of socially acceptable qualities of thought, feeling, and being—such that it is to be human.

There is much to consider when interpreting and defining self in form. Yet, doing so does not provide the depth and breadth of vision necessary to complete the masterpiece. My beliefs regarding the soul's purpose—living from the love of our Source of creation and in harmony with others—transcends any limitations imposed by individual beliefs, the beliefs that come secondary to cultural norms, societal expectations, and subscribed religious tenets, and so too my exposure to or lack thereof with such systems. One must not discount the buy-in and adherence to those systems, which is key to the experience.

One's journey to discovery of the spiritual self is a personal one. I don't mean personal in that it only happens to you, rather, personal in that it is composed of your unique experiences. The journey you undertake to spiritual awareness is highlighted by the plot points of your lived experience and earmarked with lessons individual to the self. While the lessons may be more universally or globally focused, your direct interpretation and comprehension become their micro-association.

I believe in synchronicity—the universal alignment of our human journey and those who journey with us. We awaken to many lessons through the presence and absence of individuals who appear and depart from our path. While the gifts of their presence may be blinded in obscurity, filtered through emotion, and hidden in the depths of our souls, it is our responsibility to work toward their discovery. To become intentionally present and purposeful in our lives, we must sit within these depths and acknowledge all joy, elation, love, pain, lack, and fear.

Knowing that fear often masks my ability to process my disillusionment regarding a specific person or event, I must be persistently intentional to maintain my energy, regain my center, and stand in the power of who I know myself to be. Setting intentions holds me accountable to myself, the process, and my highest good.

While the lived experience has only the meaning we assign, the truth of our being is imprinted in its very frequency, and is, therefore, unalterable—fixed and permanent. The truth of our being is the same for each of us, and I intend to make this consciousness visible.

My journey thus far has taught me many things, and I have received countless gifts because of my courage, tenacity, and resilience. When emotional responses to the external world rise within me, I am now wise enough to recognize this as a sign for me to go within and connect more deeply. Blessed by these moments of reaction, I have essentially learned to love myself and others in the way it was intended—unconditionally.

Part III

Echoes of the Spirit Within

"I am not my thoughts, emotions,
sense perceptions, and experiences.
I am not the content of my life.
I am Life. I am the space in which
all things happen. I am consciousness.
I am the Now. I Am."

—Eckhart Tolle

Channeled Wisdom

Next, I share several channeled messages I have received as guidance for our experience of Self in form. Notice some words are capitalized. This is purposeful and guided by the energies communicating the information to and through me. They refer to Knowing, Reality, Truth, Self (consciousness not in form), the Divine, the All That Is, and the Infinite I, also known as the Infinite Self or the I AM (universal consciousness).

The capitalization of these words is their reference to Universal Consciousness or the Collective of Consciousness from whom the communications are ultimately received. The information is from the part of creation, of consciousness, greater and beyond that which inhabits human form.

They also refer to knowing, reality, truth, self or self in form, and the inferior or lesser i am (consciousness in form) to differentiate between the capitalized words used on a Universal Consciousness level of frequency versus that experienced by consciousness in form or self as we perceive the human experience.

The communicators have explained we are made of the Collective of Consciousness, although our frequency is decreased and our remembrances of the lived experience muted while in perceived human form. This is intentional. When an awakening experience (awareness of Self in form) is perceived, we Know these concepts on a frequency higher than the form we inhabit. The communicators provide the distinction of words, with capitalization, to assist us in this distinction and to guard against confusion secondary to the spoken and written language used. Yes, the communicators sometimes reinforce using a capital or lowercase letter to ensure I am interpreting the information as they intend.

Please also note that, at times, the communications may include words not common to the English dictionary. This occurs secondary to the communicator's endeavors to impress upon me the meaning of the information while using language I already know. In short, sometimes words are used to convey a specific meaning, and these words are not semantically or grammatically recognized or accepted within the English language.

Q: With whom am I communicating?

A: It matters not what label you assign or what name you call us. We are all one within the Collective of Consciousness. For quite some time you have been aware of our existence and communications with you. A name to identify was not necessary; however, we are also aware of the human need to identify, and to that end, we state our connection with and through you is energetic, frequency to be exact, and will continue to be so. There is an energetic imprint or signature, if you will, impressioned upon your frequency through which you receive our communications.

We will bring information to you and through you on any occasion you choose to make available to us. There need not be a ritual or other ceremonial recognition of our sessions, rather your choice to be available is in reverence enough of the relationship we have one with the other.

That said, we do know you work best when time is scheduled and allotted. While you want to believe spontaneity and being laid back works best for you, we are aware many things go left unattended when this manner of practice is employed. Therefore, we suggest you designate a specific time each day for us to commune, as this will indeed yield the highest result for us both.

How It Began

There is truth in the writing. The assumptions and suppositions of humanity fade when we are able to come through you in this form. Although likely more tedious for you, at least presently, than other forms of communication. You experience distractions mentally that are best overcome at this time by physical writing of our thought forms. We acknowledge, Dear One, the times you are better able to receive us for those moments of connection are indeed the purest for us both. In time, we trust our communications will become a clear telepathic flow in whatever form best suites you, be it written, typed, or verbal.

We acknowledge, also, your understanding these communications will bring forward information for your growth and that of others. Currently, the writing occupies your physical self in a way that does not allow the ego self of your humanness to bleed through energetically, as it sometimes will. When this occurs, we experience the dissonance with you and have difficulty moving the conscious you out of the way so you may continue to receive. So, for in as much as this is our current method, we welcome you to our time together. We look forward to our communications with you, Dear One, and of our building a strong connection with you.

We want you to consider this time, our time, to be something of a special occasion, and we ask that you honor us and the self to the degree necessary to allow us to blend energies as regularly as possible. We have much to reveal through you and for you to share with others. You're honoring of our work and our togetherness brings a great reverence to our processes and to the sacredness of our communications. Your intention to receive us in this way will continue to sharpen and fine-tune over the course of our sessions. We are eager for the communications and our sessions, such that we will call them for now. We honor you and your willingness to acknowledge our presence. We honor your desire and openness to the concept of our existence beyond the limiting of physical presence, such as the form you currently inhabit.

Now that this matter is more formally out of the way, let us begin.

Receiving Communication

We are here and have come at this moment in your time to share with you and through you truths for you, for others. *Universal Truths* relevant to your existence in form. Relevant to the existence of all in form ready to receive our communications. *Know* being ready to receive, in a word, means the ability to hear the communication while allowing it to be what it is. Many in form, at this time, are not able to suspend judgment to accept and allow things as they are and for these individuals, this too is a part of their journey to Oneness, such that you all will have.

There is not judgment for those in form unable to get out of their own way, so to speak, for that too is a part of the discovery, the awakening, and ultimately the return to discovery of Self. This, too, shall pass. Thus, before we go further, *Know* our communications will reach those intended and in the manner intended and will be as impactful as intended. Through each individual's journey of discovery, of awareness, and insight, and most especially through the increased ability to accept and allow all things will be as intended. The communications will become *Known* on a higher level of frequency each time the individual engages with the material in any form relevant to him or her. As the journey to Self unfolds and the individual aligns higher in frequency, the communications will reveal a deeper and more profound message, also as is intended. Let us move forward.

To *Know* Self in form requires insight and awareness of the frequency within. If nothing else, a curiosity or desire to know more beyond that which one currently perceives as self. Motivation to explore the concepts and foundational aspects perceived to be self. The you of known self and the knowingness of self on a broader scale can be, for many, an intimidating concept. *Know* the human journey, to be self in form, is not for the timid. Rather, it is an arduous undertaking of challenges placed in one's path for the purpose of acquiring knowledge, skill, and the ability to move through them despite the almost insurmountable nature of things one encounters along the way. Understand that what one experiences as difficult or challenging is perceived as easily overcome by another.

Life is not about comparison or competition. Yet, if one must make it so, then intentionally focus on being a better self than you were previously so the All of Humanity comes out ahead. The purpose of the lived experience is to develop the ability to perceive more keenly, to discern more adeptly, and to acquire lessons more readily—all of which lead to the Knowing of Self in form as the All That Is. For this to ultimately come to fruition requires many things occurring synchronously across the lived experience and the integration of the events and experiences in a manner consistent with continued growth and development. That's it!

While the lived experience may appear, at times, a daunting undertaking, it is one of the most joyous occasions for the self. To *be* as self in form is miraculous, and to discover Self as the impetus of one's very existence even more so. The energetic frequency of being human is, in and of itself, unparalleled. We acknowledge there are many situations and conditions impacting the human self, which can significantly hinder or otherwise impede one's discovery of the Truths regarding Self in form. So too, these are necessary components of the lived experience. The perceived incumbrances are how one is faced, for lack of a better term, with events and occurrences from which to acquire what is necessary for growth. What one learns, how one learns it, and the direction he or she takes with the acquired knowledge results in one's individuality of the lived experience. We are often more excited about your existence in form than the individual can perceive, and this is largely due to our Knowing of the outcome for the All of Humanity. It can be difficult to observe the challenges and hardships with which those in form are faced. The experience of dissonant frequency resonance is observed by all. Rest assured, we are here to support and encourage the best way forward for each of you, and we gladly do so with love unconditional—for that and only that is love.

The Potentiality of Being Human

We acknowledge the All of Humanity, as a whole, and the resonance of your unified oneness, despite the separations you all hold one with the other. We honor how you each choose to exhibit individually, yet we do not see or experience you the same way. In the totality of your existence, we observe you each individually and as a part of the Greater Whole. The oneness of your beingness. En masse, the energetic experience of you, of others, of the All of Humanity is quite an honor to behold. So much potential within all of you. We know this may present as judgmental, and it is not intended in that way. We are merely presenting the overall bigger picture, as it were, of the humanity we experience. And, with that, we acknowledge the strivings of many to Know the Self in a different way than presently perceived. These individuals are no more and no less than others. We say these individuals are simply aligning on a different convergence. One that is very much required for the ultimate survival of you all as there is a continued evolution of sorts through the lived experience, the acting out of your characters, and the performances in which you each engage throughout your experiences of individuality and as a part of the totality of humanity.

In this form, your present form, much can and will be experienced. Your physical self allows for the perceptions of being on many energetic levels, the least of which is physical. We acknowledge, too, your place in any given experience and that your present form places an inordinate amount of importance on the physicality of your being rather than the energetic connections to the processes as they are perceived.

If you can, and so choose to, allow the self to be experienced as waves of energy. Perpetual, infinite, unimpeded flow of being. How does experiencing Self in this way differ, for you, from a focus on the mere physicalness of existence? We encourage you each day to sit in this space, the energy of identified Self, and allow it to be unimpeded by thought, by body, by the business of being human that consumes so much of your day-to-day experiences.

We acknowledge the need of the human experience. It serves as a vessel through which to access the Energetic Self in a different way. A form of experience required by you and others presently that best suits your level of assimilation with the Greater Whole. The Totality of Oneness. We honor this experience you are involved with presently and choose to work with and through you now with the understanding our connection is intended to deepen as communications become regular.

Next, we will communicate our intention of these teachings. Firstly, we honor you with the highest of reverence for your insight, curiosity, and willingness to strive for a connection with us. We acknowledge the quirkiness of humanity. Everyone striving to be different, set apart from each other, and the motivations to be acknowledged as above, better or separate in some form. By now, many of you realize this, recognize its futility and desire a way forward that honors collaboration and cooperation as the fuel for continued existence and, ultimately, the evolution of humanity.

Those inhabiting your Earth are about 50:50 when it comes to awareness of the situation at hand, of the brokenness—for lack of a better term—of the way in which life is currently carried out. Approximately half of humanity is oblivious to the underpinnings of Reality and the Truth of existence. These are the individuals who work to survive and call it living. Those who cannot seem to create a meaningful identity flounder with addiction, engage in activities that go against established laws, and so on. These are also the individuals who are at the opposite end of the spectrum. Highly motivated to achieve, to succeed, to arrive and be acknowledged as better and somehow separate from and in ways above the whole. Your world requires both, just in better balance, to ensure continued opportunities for enlightenment and growth.

We said approximately half existed in the way we just described, and we will reinforce it as approximately half at present. That leaves the approximate half who are experiencing, seeking to experience, or who are at least aware and desirous of life or the perception thereof to be enhanced somehow. Not by fame, financial wealth, or the struggle perceived as necessary to overcome or rise above for the experience to have meaning. Rather, these individuals acknowledge—on some level—and we will tell you it is an energetic awareness of Self that exists outside the physical self but is experienced through the senses and physical mind as consciousness of being.

Now, we will tell you, Shelley, our Scribe, is no great scientist with hypotheses related to human existence. While we acknowledge her understandings via education and learning at a funicular level, it is not and was not necessary to allow the communications we bring through her. We acknowledge the journey of self she is undertaking, as are you all, and we will make use of her understandings and the information she has gathered throughout this experience, just as we would and do with others who also receive us.

Simply put, intelligence is not so much a factor in all of this—our communication—as is the desire to be open to the possibility of it all and the dedication to sit with us and to serve as our voice, if you will, for lack of a better way to communicate what it is we will be accomplishing during our sessions.

In fact, while Shelley is intellectual enough to question, and please know this can get in the way of and slow down our communications, she is also curious and possesses a sense of wonder and awe about this whole process. We will tell you, her fears of being observed as fraudulent, phony, and hokey (her word for it) do cause significant dissonance, at times, in our ability to connect and communicate.

There is great pressure to perform at high levels within your experience, and this is off-putting for individuals who swim upstream, as it were. Individuals such as she honor truth and value connection. It is important to her others feel energetically comfortable before proceeding, yet the intellectual self comprehends this is not guaranteed and is ultimately out of the scope of her ability to control. Which, we will tell you, is from where her greatest hesitation and resistance arises. Her desire to connect, inquisitiveness, and motivation to achieve this process is constantly at odds with the fears created and upheld by the society in which she lives. Perseverance is key.

BEING OF SERVICE

There is nothing we can tell you that is not already held within the awareness of your Universal Consciousness. The responsibility is yours to develop the abilities to access this information. Development of the skills necessary to consistently access information accurately and with the depth required to bring it forth requires consistent work on your part.

When you are one with the Creator there is a resonant alignment of frequency. Through alignment in frequency, you Claim your right to its presence. Through Claiming you are then ascending in frequency. As your frequency becomes more aligned with that of the Creator, you open to possibilities beyond which you currently comprehend as your reality. The world before you is that of which you have created.

There is a desire within you to be of service. We say of service, meaning your approach to bring information to others. However, we are not necessarily overtaken with the claims you make in coming forward. It appears you present as though service is the main goal, yet we understand that beneath this is a desire to be known, to be admired, to be revered. You must understand that this is of the ego and is not being of service to your Higher Self, your spiritual journey, or that of others.

We are not saying that the information would not be pertinent to those whom you serve. We are saying the information will be more well-received when it comes from a place without ego for you. It is not wrong to desire notoriety or acknowledgment, but to seek Divinity through service when driven by the ego is not creating space in which to elevate to your highest self.

There is good within you, and it shall be brought forward when you are able to heal forward—when you heal through that which you still claim. The experiences in the life you are currently having weigh heavily upon you in many areas. While you may believe you are consciously aware of those areas and their impact, trust us, you are not.

Complete awareness of that which holds you in the darkness would of itself be freeing from those things. While these things continue to pull you into humanness, Know you can transcend them and move forward in your spiritual development by proclaiming an intention to set them free and experience life from your Source Self–that of a love vibration in human form and the presence you currently inhabit. The world before you will rejoice with this Claiming of Self.

There is much spiritual wisdom and learned knowledge within you that you have come into this life with and was acquired through your actions in this incarnation. Please know we are here to work with you as you move through this life with the intention to transform and transmute that which does not serve your Highest Good, your True Self, the Divine Self within.

Challenge is the impetus for personal growth. Your uncomfortableness with a situation is encouraging you to rise above things and discover new ways to be present within the self. You cannot be in the light while allowing other things to hold you in darkness, meaning that which you fear is in the darkness and you cannot live in the light while tethered to things within the darkness, such as your anxiety about getting old. All things will be revealed through these processes; they cannot be otherwise.

BRINGERS OF LIGHT

You are light, a bringer of light, each of you. The potential to exude this light is within you all. While there appear to be discrepancies between you, and you see each other as different in many ways—this, too, is an illusion.

The shroud of illusion is over most of humanity, but this veil is lifting. Disillusionment over the various identified separations is growing and soon will overtake the All of Humanity. We use the word humanity to encapsulate humankind in its entirety, rather than the verb form with which to describe the all of you, as that is clearly in a state of lack within many cultures throughout your world.

When we say the veil is lifting, we refer to the increasing awareness by many of Self in form. This is no small undertaking. All of you have spent hundreds, if not thousands of your lifetimes to reach this place. Yet, for you, it feels as if you have always known. And yes, that is how it is intended to be–awakening to the awareness of Self.

While many are led astray by various distractions, the biggest of which is your concepts of religion, such that it is practiced and professed today. More and more of you will discover the Light within self. To that end, more and more of you will move away from being controlled through fear and will instead move toward and into a place of Knowing within self that captivates curiosity and motivates exploration of the not yet remembered.

Your re-remembering will occur in whatever way best suits your needs at the time and in accordance with that which can be best tolerated by your individual level of acceptance. It does one no good to be flooded with information when the individual is in a space of non-acceptance, fear, compliance, or is otherwise disengaged from Self. There must be a level of curiosity and openness to such things, for the awareness to spurn further action. While skepticism can be a protection mechanism, it can be a deterrent to further seeking Truth of oneself.

Know that each of you experiences countless obstacles and setbacks along the path to your remembering, or awakening, if you will. The least of which is physical death of the form you inhabit. Returning in form is the process by which each of you continues to further the Knowing of Self, and through the experiences unique to that version of life gifted during time in form. The challenges have been purported by many as the teachers and bringers of Knowledge for self. The true lessons are not the experiences, rather how each individual responds to the challenge presented. Just as wisdom is experienced by the internalizing of knowledge, so too is the growth of Self encouraged by the actions of Self in form.

The undertaking of life is not an easy path to Knowing, but it is a necessary one. Rest assured, you are ALL on this path, and while it may appear the science experiment, as our Scribe calls it, has gone horribly wrong—you are ALL exactly where you are intended to be at any given point within your existence in form.

Universal Love

et us begin where we left off, but first, a reminder: Sitting with us regularly will yield greater opportunities for communication.

We continue by addressing the concepts of Universal Love, such that our Scribe calls it. She is correct, in part, there is no need for us to label things such that you do. We exist as we are. We know of our being, our intention, our lineage. It is the Energetic Self in form that must identify, label, and make sense of us, of existence, of the existence of the unseen and the unknown. And well you should, if nothing else but to form a common language.

It would benefit all in form to learn to accept what is, without question and that is not the nature and intent of your purpose, such that it is at this time. Future incarnations (your term) of inhabitants in form will come into form Knowing their position and purpose. A blade of grass does not question its existence or purpose, yet it is alive nonetheless.

Each of you now has come to Known the Self in form in a specific way. The way you identify is limiting. Yes, we acknowledge the form you inhabit has physical limitations to the extent you believe them to exist. And, too, the limitations are very real to the degree the form itself is capable of only so much.

When you inhabit form, there is an understanding it will create barriers to the experience of Self that are grounded in the physicality of being in this way. You accept these challenges as a part of the experience and for the lessons such barriers bring to the Knowing of Self in the specific form you inhabit. Across the variable lifetimes of existence in form, you come to Know many things and collectively add to the Knowingness of the Whole, specifically to the concepts of Self in form for your existences and experiences. After all, this is your journey. A voyage to Self that would not be possible without inhabiting form.

To address fully the concept of Universal Love, the energy of the Whole, The All, one must merely accept that it is. The range of frequency is experienced with much awe and trepidation, for lack of a better term, by those in form. There is ignorance of the intricacies of energetic flow within all things, just as there is curiosity and reverence.

Those who have come before you and the Self you have been previous to now—as aware, such that form experiences awareness as an almost tangible entity—as it were. Truth or proof of a thing. In short, to accept is to believe. To allow deepens awareness. There are many blocks experienced by those in form, the least of which is acceptance. We say acceptance is to believe to assist your Knowing of a thing, an occurrence, a possibility for Truth, for this is the birthplace of Awareness.

Awareness of the Whole can only come with acceptance. You must first allow the concept to be as it is, without question or query. The inquisitive nature often not acknowledged or brought into Reality of form is the root of where the processes can become impeded.

Acceptance of what is as it is does not require understanding. This is an almost impossible concept for those in form to grasp. Conditioned to query the whys and what fors, the circle of attempts to understand is born. Once entrapped within this framework, True Acceptance is lost.

The conditioned response of form serves a purpose as the requirements of form become more. In its early stages, form does not possess the ability—at least not the language of communication required to express the inquisitiveness that comes with moving through the processes that accompany moving through being in form. The experience begins merely being. The rest comes as form experiences the journey.

Form, as an infant, does not question why a thing or an experience is pleasant or unpleasant, why it occurs or does not occur. It accepts the occurrence of said thing as is. What goes on behind the scenes for the developing intellectual, emotional, and physical of the form is another discussion.

In the aforesaid manner, form as an infant accepts what is as it is, thereby allowing it to exist. Through the allowing of what is, there is rudimentary understanding. The seeking to understand with query becomes a process of the developing form. In the beginning, there was accepting and allowing.

Unlimited Self

You are infinite, limited only by form.

Those who have chosen to experience Self in form have done so to acquire a perspective unavailable by other means, no matter how brief the time in form exists. Through experience in form, several insights, if you will, can be achieved. Key to this decision is benevolence, humility, compassion, and learning to live in form as the expression of Self. Therein lies the difficulty of this undertaking. If all humanity lived as Self in form, there would be no need for continued experience. As there is suffering in form of man's own doing, there too shall be the experience of the overcoming of it.

Self without form is without the trappings encountered when one experiences life as human, the underpinnings of which are paramount to one's experiences in relation to others in form, the individual, and the Collective as a Whole.

In form, you have the ability to choose experiences and outcomes, although the great majority are blissfully unaware of these options, thus falling victim to self. For those, the experience of form can present as a daunting and unrelenting turn of events, if you will. Without the awareness of Self in form and the curiosity to explore the possibility of such, being human is practically a lesson in futility. Literally and figuratively.

Those in form spend many, many lives in this state of unawareness. Even though many will begin to have an awareness of Self within form, societies are conditioned to believe generational dogma that requires them to remain in compliance with pre-ordained schemas or the self suffers judgment and ridicule, and is often ostracized by others of kind.

Know this is all created in fear. It is an excellent way to control the masses and to inhibit further curiosity and awareness. The human drive to fit in and be accepted is rarely overpowered by curiosity and wonder. Should more in form choose curiosity, inquisitiveness, and to follow the path less taken, infinity of Knowing would be available to them.

At this juncture is where those in form, such as you, are integral to the part of the process of awakening, as many prefer to call it. Although it is not truly an awakening, as much as it is a remembering, if you will, of Self. When this is acquired, all things are possible. As we initially said, you are infinite, limited only by form.

This is where we will leave off for today. Thank you for heeding our encouragement to establish connection to further our ability to blend with you.

SELF

The you identified as self is not the real or true Self. Rather, it is a representation of your perceptions and conditioned beliefs of self and how it is expected to be; and we say be to initiate your comprehension of the true Self within the physical form inhabited as self. You are one with the body you inhabit.

The individuation of the physical form is an illusory separation-the unnecessary parsing of symbiotic energies-experiencing one through the other. The understanding of which is limited prior to one's awareness of the True Self. The Self of the Creator, the True Self, of which all is made, and through which all is connected, is the energy present within the physical embodiment of self and that which makes differentiation possible.

To facilitate realization of Self as infinite energy, currently in body, we offer the following related concepts: the human self is the inferior 'i' (lesser 'I') otherwise known as the inferior self or the i am; and energy of the Creator, present with all living things is the infinite 'I' (greater 'I'), otherwise known as the Infinite Self or the I AM.

Speaking of self in this way allows differentiation between the limitedness of the physical embodiment inferior self i am and the infinite I AM that exists beyond limitation. The differences between the inferior, lesser self and the Infinite Self are vast, yet not necessarily complicated.

Largely, the inferior self experience is of response and reaction from a perspective of conditioned thought, emotion, and behavior. Primarily seeking self-preservation, the inferior self strives to acquire and maintain control over everything from involuntary bodily functions to its own thoughts and environment. Conversely, the Infinite Self is not limited by such constraints, to include the concepts of space and time the inferior self has been conditioned to perceive and thereby experience.

LOVE AS FREQUENCY

What this is not is love as a human emotion, experienced as a feeling toward or about something. Your kind has a long-standing history of expressing emotion through feeling words. For many, emotions and feelings have become synonymous, which we will tell you they are not. Emotions are experienced within and around you as the energy of your system, your Energetic Self. Feelings are the words you assign to these energetic experiences.

When you can separate the Energetic Self and the physical self, by language and by thought, you are better able to comprehend the vastness of their separateness. We do not intend to separate the two, as if they do not or should not coexist, in fact, they must for your purposes in form. But because you are only accustomed to experiencing the self as an integration of the two, it can be almost unfathomable to believe you can know them as separate and independent one from the other.

We are to inform you that is the purpose of this discussion before you now. For the you to which you are accustomed to progress forward with these concepts you are required, as much as you are able, to begin to distinguish between the two in explicit and clearly defined ways. Physical. Energetic. Yes, combined to harmoniously create the you of historical and current experience, yet gloriously independent.

Interdependence and independence are two concepts we must define for you now, as not everyone understands with certainty what exactly is meant by each. We will tell you, independence in a system is its manner of existing, in present state, without a reliance on other systems. Interdependence relies on the existence and seamless blending of other systems for its harmonious integration.

The human condition, for example, is an interdependent system. Consider the physical self. It is not merely DNA turned into flesh and bone. The human self is comprised of energetic, chemical, physical, and environmental processes that come together like a well-choreographed and continuous dance. Each system influences the other synchronously coming together in what is experienced as you.

Can you now see the implications of observing self as merely one unit, either physical or energetic? It is a large disservice to the capability of the entire system to possess such a limited perspective of self and that of your fellows.

LIFE

We are here to inform you that life, your life, the life you believe is transpiring is not as it may seem. While yes, you are alive, as it were, and a living and breathing organism, the terminology of life such that you know it is not all that it may appear.

We encourage you to not get bogged down with terminology or to become quagmired in the sciences. Rather, allow the possibility of other Realities to exist through you as you exist. We understand this is something new to which you must become accustomed, and for many, will not yet be attainable. However, with persistence, patience, and practice, you will be able to move aside that knowingness of what you currently believe to be existence, to receive information from another Source.

That said, we also encourage you to sit within and ground into your system of faith, such that it is your practice. Not in a manner so strictly that outside influences are not possible, rather in the possibility of limitless oneness and a belief in a greater plan for all mankind, all humankind as it were.

We request of you now, to allow the experience of witness to rest with you. In the role as a witness, you are more open to suggested thought forms and alternate realities. We are not suggesting abandonment of self here, which is what our Scribe is now focused on. And, diplomatically so, she is keenly aware that humanity holds steadfast to several belief systems that may be difficult to challenge, most especially when you become entrenched in the rightness and wrongness of what we are asking when compared to your belief systems as they currently exist.

We are not intending to bring information in opposition to what you already know or believe to know. Rather, we offer an adjunct to your current reality to be incorporated into your knowingness as you are able. Being able to assume information into your awareness takes great courage and trust on your part. We also know the acquisition of information must be relevant and meaningful to the organism to which it is being introduced. We are not speaking of indoctrinating you, or anyone in humanity, with preposterous notions regarding other life forms or alien nations, although be aware this is a discussion for another time.

In this moment, now, we are asking you to step back from conscious scrutiny just enough to allow the possibility of "what if," as our Scribe would say. Allow your emotional and intellectual selves to blend coherently, with the knowingness and safety required to be present yet allowing.

This is the state one must achieve to invite what we are imparting. Safe, yet distanced, as if observing the self in process through a window. You are present, yes. You are aware, yes. You are safe and capable of removing self from this process at any time you so desire. We are merely here to guide you in the discovery of our information on a level above that of the intellectual consciousness you hold as truth presently.

We will instruct you now to breathe deeply several times. With each exhalation, releasing apprehension, fear, and any requirements for control over what is about to take place. With each inhalation, knowing you are safe within your home or whatever space you now occupy. With this knowingness, we encourage you to continue breathing into the physical self, into your awareness of self, and into the space we are creating and holding for you. Our presence is with you at whatever time you choose to partake in this work.

Materialism

Many things can be achieved by observing you. Not you as an individual, rather you as a collective species. Much energy is expended in the gathering of things. We marvel at the effort and energy you put forth in acquiring, naming, and valuing things. It is unnecessary for your existence to have so many things, but you collectively agree they are necessary; and, because of this, you continue to strive to acquire.

Interestingly, there never seems to be enough for most of you. When you achieve what you believe you needed or wanted, there is always more that is left desired. Yet somehow even those who have achieved, acquired, and amassed a great many things, still have not reached the level of accolade they desire. One would think the acquisition of many things would become less popular, instead the inverse is true. The less people have, the more people want, and the more people have, the more they want—despite an awareness of unfulfillment amongst all of their things.

Man has long assigned value to possessions and property. Not so long ago, man assigned value to his possession of other people. Thankfully this has fallen away in most parts of your world. A resurgence can be seen in what is currently happening around your world with the buying and selling of individuals.

The disregard of human suffering imposed by other humans, and the ability of the masses to remain disconnected one from the other only serves to contribute to your separateness.

It is through this lack of identification that you, mankind as a species, are able to impose these atrocities one upon the other and upon the animals that inhabit your world. Mankind has long suffered and will continue to do so until the Awakening of all. While awakening is occurring for many of your kind, it is progressing much slower than we had hoped. Although the number of those in process is highly commendable, we continue our presence with intent to impact more greatly than the numbers now allow.

There are a great many of you already Awakened and in process. It is these of you who will lead the others forward in process. The Awakened ones are those who shine light for others in process. To be in process means many and varied things, the most basic of which is one's awareness of embodiment.

Awareness of embodiment is the beginning of Awakening. We call the process Awakening, as this is Universally understood to be a process of coming into a new awareness. While there is no physical movement from one state to another, there is movement of one's awareness through various states of being and intention. Often referred to as enlightenment, Awakening occurs in many ways and is always expanding through steps or levels, if you will, of the receiver's knowingness and understanding of multiple processes—both human and energetic.

REALITY

The you that you think you are does not exist. At least not such that you think, believe, and perceive it does. In fact, the reality you cling to as the very basis of evidence for everything you do is, as well, not real in the sense of Truth being Reality. Truth, defined, we say is the energetic existence of beingness that is not held primarily in the physical form, nor is it representative of the potential the energy possesses. Rather, Truth, yes with a capital T, is the Source of all things, and your definition of reality has, in past renditions, indicated it as fact when it is not.

Reality only exists on an energetic level. While there is Reality interspersed within and around you and your physical self, you can ever only experience Reality as energy, as frequency, as Truth. When one allows self to experience the energetic beingness, which is available to all, we say you are then able to Know Truth.

While we agree there is necessity for the existence of the physical self and the cognitive self, these are largely functions of process to facilitate Awareness more efficiently. In physical form, you, at least the you of known perception, engage in interactions and have experiences with others of your kind, animals, and their environment. These experiences offer insights and impart information on an energetic scale often undetected.

It has been our experience such detections are rather easily explained away as coincidence, déjà vu, and synchronicity, despite the energetic nature. We cannot and do not hold your kind as accountable as we likely should. There is reason to give leave when you honestly do not know any better. If you were energetically aware and advanced, this discussion would be moot. As it is not, we will continue.

Reality and Truth are the subjects of today's communication. Truth, the energetic beingness of All, uses the physical to experience, and that which you perceive as self, is the awareness of these experiences. Should you choose to understand Reality from this perspective, accepting Truth will facilitate this kindlier for you.

Reality, we say, is the concept of all beingness as experienced through you and the expression of which you portray in action through your physical presence. Reality can only be experienced in this way. To do so otherwise would be a false experience and a misrepresentation of Truth, such as we described.

Density of Spirit

We are with you always in ALL ways. Clarification of ALL is required, as you immediately go to us showing up in the shower, and yes, while we are there too, your modesty and privacy is not at issue with us as much as it is with you. Many of you seem to believe we see as you do, with physical eyes, and that just is not so. We Know your energy. Again, capital k Know, to accentuate the relationship and the depth of Knowingness beyond that of the intellectual mind of your experience.

We sense and Know you as energy, and do not perceive you with vision, as a physical form which you have identified. We Know you, individually, and others, in a mass energy way. Rather, you are an energetic presence with a unique imprint in your frequency, much like a human fingerprint, if you will, that sets you apart in frequency from your counterparts. Your energy emits the same frequency as others in spirit and has a ringtone unique to you.

Density of the physical self is an adjustment, at least initially. For some, the transition takes considerably longer. We are certain each of you has experienced or heard of someone who has commented that they "just don't feel like myself." Perhaps you've even heard someone say, "I don't feel like I belong here." Maybe it was you. The feeling of presence, as an energetic being, blended with a physical self can be disconcerting. Especially when the individual's experience of self is closely connected with his spiritual presence. In such instances, being in form can feel off-putting, foreign, and disingenuous to the experience of self.

Being Human

The journey of the human self is an arduous one, often tedious for seekers and those who are Awakening, for these individuals experience things more deeply, energetically, and therefore emotionally than their non-awakening or less progressed in Awakening counterparts. Seekers of Truth, yes capital T Truth, which emphasizes the importance of it as being a Divinely guided Reality of self.

Your continued growth, that of our Scribe, and others as well, is a requirement of the Ascension of the All of Humanity. We use the word humanity as encompassing each and every human on your Earth. This word, when used by us in this way, is imbued with the Knowingness and compassion void of judgment and categorization. We acknowledge each human as a part of the Greater Whole and recognize the Light within each of you. The Light is how we see you and each other. We recognize the energetic patterning housed within each human form, and you are to know each is distinct yet similar.

Regardless of the human aspect, his or her deeds and accomplishments in form, we see each as they are—energy—and our acknowledgment of you all with the compassion deserving of Soul is as it is intended. Humanity is an inclusive term often used and a level of reverence and solemnity when you and your peers, at least those who are more aware, speak about your Earth, societies, and inhabitants and the exploitations taking place globally. It is as much an endearment as it is a plea for more peaceful unity amongst you all.

Our session today will focus on these concepts of self as different than and separate from the whole.

Unification of the Whole

Part of the human experience, incarnation if you will, is to unify the Whole. While there are countless theories regarding the origins of humanity and the purpose for its being, the business of this distraction keeps you focused on seeking to understand rather than accepting what is. There is a vast difference between the two.

Your intellect was intended to question, query, and to use exploration as a tool to discover Greater Truths. The issues that arise, however, are primarily driven by the intellectual self, which is also focused on preservation of the self. Overlaid with the conditioning of society, culture, religion, politics, and the generational perspectives lain before you—accepted as Truth—without question and worn like a tailored coat by the masses, those impediments, strivings, and distractions do little more than offer the intellect a series of mental gymnastics to keep it occupied.

True Freedom awaits each of you. It is not achieved when the Energetic Self leaves its human form, rather when each of you accepts awareness of Self as being part of the Greater

Whole without the need and hindrance of understanding on an intellectual, conscious mind level.

Now, we will tell you, acceptance of this magnitude sets off red flags for most of humanity. Even without reaching a conclusion, those who have all pondered his or her existence developed an ideal, an acceptable thought form to appease this curiosity of knowing on some level. While the conclusion itself may be somewhat flexible, mutable, and not fully developed, the conscious self requires a form of acceptable resolution—a belief on which to base future determinations, decisions, and potential outcomes—without which these would be true chaos amongst you.

Imagine for a moment if every human on Earth believed life was a one-way trip to nowhere, that the ride had no purpose, and that the end was final. One pass through. One chance to do, see, and be, all for the unknown duration of the experience.

In such a scenario, would self-awareness, integrity, collaborative and cooperative means seek the ultimate end together? Or would the individual seek to gain self-fulfillment at almost any consequence? When would cost to the self become great enough to regulate selfishness of the individual? What would such a world look like?

You all benefit from the varied levels of awareness and ascension co-existing and co-inhabiting your Earth at any given time. Each of you cannot be in the same place within your development, for it is encounters and experiences with others that offer opportunity for your growth.

If each of you were at the same level, struggling through the process of enlightenment and ascension at exactly the same place at the same time, you would all be in chaos, and the promises of Utopia would not exist as they would be unfathomable to your conscious awareness.

That said, we acknowledge humanity's similarity throughout various periods of existence. However, we spotlight the advancements born from individuality, out-of-the-box processes, and those willing to step out of the struggle to conceive a different way of being.

We also acknowledge these perceived advancements are not to a benefit of the Greater Whole—including the Earth—at a rate of approximately half. The advancements are, however, of great necessity for future developments for one cannot occur without the other. There must be trial and error, failure, and defeat to move ever so slightly in the direction of advancement toward any cause or effect of change. As a whole, humanity, for the most part, has mastered trial and error as the advancement of civilizations across your world have made similar advances within an approximation of the same identified era. This is no coincidence.

ONENESS

Today, let us continue our previous topic of unity, the oneness of the All of Humanity, as this is of utmost importance for your intellectual understanding and, of course, integration for your energetic awareness.

The complexity created by the blending of the Self, the Energetic Self, and the physical aspects of the body is as great as it is simplistic. The two, for the most part, simply co-exist. However, when you go deeper into these aspects of self, you will discover subtle energetic differences. The density of the body is almost consumed by the aliveness of its processes. Yet, your awareness of these processes would not exist without the Energetic Self's beingness within the body.

Can the physical self exist without integration of the Energetic Self? We say most certainly yes. The body is a vessel, a living organism composed of chemical and electrical processes that are very much independent of the Soul. These processes would occur automatically, instinctually, to ensure—as much as possible—the preservation of the small self. We say small self not with an intent to lessen or make less of the physical body but to begin presenting the difference between the physical self and the energetic being—the Greater Self. The words we use are limited by the values placed on them and can cause confusion when applied in ways outside of the presentation in which they are given by us as intended. Do you understand this?

The transitioning of understanding from the small self and Greater Self must occur in a succinct manner to create awareness of both while holding each in the reverence of its whole, as intended.

Each of you exists in this way—as physical self, or body, in which the Greater Self, the Energetic Self or Soul is housed. Our Scribe learned several years ago a helpful distinction that appears to work well for individuals who experience difficulty with this concept.

After a new awareness of Self, following a session in which another energetic being affected her physical self, she had the distinct experience of the separateness and the co-occurring unity of her physical body, her Energetic Self, and the other nonphysical energy moving through her systems. She experienced a clear distinction between body, mind, spirit, as it were. This was a profound awareness for her on all levels and she spent several days acclimating to this new awareness. We recall how she marveled at the details of her physical self. Everything from her fingers, eyes, and skin to her ability to walk, digest food and convert it to energy to sustain the body, her ability to grow new life and birth children, and the aging process. She voraciously devoured information on the human body and its processes as if reading an owner's manual.

She pondered many of these age-old theories and hypothesized several new ones of her own. It was a grand Awareness, and we observed much growth in her during this time. The takeaway was her ability to accept and integrate everything on a level of inclusivity as a cohesive whole. She became profoundly aware of the distinction between the physical self and its ability to exist without the Energetic Self, as does any organism. The great awareness was that of her Energetic Self, which exists independent of the body. The awareness deepened profoundly once this distinction became known to her conscious self. For her, this experience was necessary and a deliberate part of her awakening.

The takeaway is that after this experience, even before her research and integration of all she became aware, our Scribe clearly made the distinction of the Energetic Self inhabiting the physical form. She began referring to the body as "my human." This designation, a loving awareness and an embracing of both aspects of self has resulted in a splendid unity between the two.

While each could exist without the other, awareness and integration of both allow for a deeper connection and acceptance of the Reality of Truth. Together, consciousness, outside of intellectual understanding, exists, and only when blended is there an opportunity for a deeper awareness of Self.

The physical body must exist for the Energetic Self to be housed within, as we have said, while either exists independent of the other when combined intellectual consciousness exits. When an individual has full awareness of the body as a separate entity, independent from yet dependent on the Energetic or Soul Self for consciousness of being, then Consciousness outside intellect and reasoning of the physical mind can exist.

The Soul's awareness of inhabiting the body exists; however, is not concerned with this as much as you may like to believe. While the human self often ponders and hypothesizes, contemplates, and seeks to understand and make sense of the self in all its facets as well as the world it inhabits—the Soul Knows. It Knows of its own existence, is aware of its history and future concurrently, and does not toil with the matters of the intellect such that the physical self does.

In the larger scope of things, you require an understanding of sorts to alleviate the busyness of the mind in so much as it is necessary to the process of opening the awareness. The physical self first requires understanding. This is the function of the integrations prior to Awareness.

As such, we offer you this. Review your knowledge and understanding of other animal species inhabiting the Earth. Lions, sharks, horses, snakes, cats, dogs, cows, pigs, chickens, elephants, hippopotamuses, and various species of birds and insects. None of these animals has continued to evolve in the way of the human.

Yes, we acknowledge animals and plants adapt to environmental impacts as well as adapting to evolutionary impacts and have, in ways, evolved over their time in existence. However, none of their evolutionary accomplishments parallel that of the human. In comparison, other species have evolved to exist, and the majority of their existence is focused on survival.

In contrast, the human has evolved in massive ways due to its intellect. This does not mean nonhuman plant and animal life does not possess a level of intelligence unique to its species. The point we are making is that in an advancement of self aspects, the human far exceeds any other species on Earth. this is not a distinction made as a comparison of better/worse or good/bad, merely an exercise for you to begin to gain insight and acknowledge the accomplishment of the human as a species.

Despite all it has accomplished, the similarities and differences clearly marked throughout the records of your history, the human experience cannot fulfill one's Soul purpose without awareness of its existence. Integration requires both awareness and a blending of the two—the physical and the energetic (Soul).

We will pose a new perspective at this time. Our acknowledgment of your evolution includes the words used to represent the various aspects and understanding that have been acquired. One of which we can agree is the concept of the lesser i am, meaning the physical human self and the Soul housed within, and the distinction of this with the greater I AM, referring to the Universal Consciousness.

Moving forward, we will use this in reference to the human self and Soul Self versus the Knowingness of Universal Consciousness and your existence as a part of the Greater Whole. We will use the terms interchangeably in reference.

Knowing

If we are to sit one with the other, a commitment to the process is necessary. There is a reverence of our sessions that requires you to be present, uninterrupted if possible. That is why you experience the urgency so early in the morning. The agreement we made for this to occur was noticeably the opportune period of your day when you are less distracted and more likely to be present as is needed for our communications.

With regard to connectivity, we are working with you energetically to establish connection, which requires of us and you a great change in frequency. We continue to develop this with you in this way.

We welcome you to this session; let us begin.

During our most recent time together, the conclusion of our communication was not complete, and we wish to finish it at this time before moving on. We spoke to the energetic aspect of your being in somewhat greater detail than perhaps some prefer; however, this is indeed necessary with the level of awareness intended to be touched by the information as we presently address humanity as one, and there are a great number who are not yet in their Knowing of Self.

To be in one's Knowing of Self is not finality; it is perhaps a beginning. We acknowledge there are many with a deeper

Knowing, this is not the case such that is required for the shift to occur. As we previously indicated, all levels of awareness are a necessary and integral part of the transition.

Now, as much as our Scribe is open to the concepts presented, we do at times share a greater perspective with her to satisfy her intellectual self by showing her images of the Earth's position in your named galaxy and universe and what is beyond it. This humbles her and pauses her persistent "what if" approach. Inquisitiveness is necessary as much as it can be a hindrance. She remains open to our sessions.

The Energetic Self and the conscious awareness of the human form are one in the same. It exists within each of you, until the physical can no longer serve in this capacity. Together, the two engage in a symbiotic relationship. The caveat is, in or out of physical form, the Energetic Self retains information—the history of self. The physical form exists and is alive, however, the Energetic Self within allows for consciousness—awareness of self. Arguably, the physical can exist without this awareness, as it is a magnificent creation of chemical and energetic exchanges and relays. Truly a marvel to behold. In your case, that was not the intent of the design, if you will.

Your physical form, such that it now exists, was intended as a vessel for the Energetic Self or at least a part of it. Understandably, the body is dense and is therefore heavier in vibration and frequency than the Energetic Self. The blending of these energies is a process most do not recall. While there are those who do, they can tell you the assimilation is not an arduous or painful process. This is due, in part, to the Soul's Knowingness. The awareness of self in previous embodiment allows for the assimilation process to be a smoother transition.

Some individuals experience a hiccup, if you will, when the early stages of human development come into being and the individual has retained access to his or her awareness of being alive in another period of existence on Earth. This is not commonplace, however, it does occur, and we will tell you when this occurs it is real, true, and correct.

Individuals who speak their awareness of such existence, for lack of a better term, are often viewed through a lens of disbelief and responded to out of fear: fear of the unknown, fear of judgment, fear of being observed or labeled as different.

Sadly, it is not the Truth of all to possess this awareness. Such individuals are on your Earth to shine a light, if you will, to open a door to the possibility of existence beyond the known and accepted norm of the physical presently experienced.

We can say, quite often, the hindrance of such revelations comes at the hand of his or her fellows—individuals striving to understand, to quantify and qualify the experience rather than accepting it as is. And, when the individual making the claim is other than a developing human, by this we mean a child versus an adult, it is more often likely he or she will be identified as having some form of affliction with the mental or cognitive capacities.

Each inhabitant is equipped with the Energetic Self. Within its physical form, the processes of physical form and Energetic Self blend and become the You of known existence. The awareness of self as both physical and energetic can take some adjustment and explanation. We said the earlier this process can be identified and Claimed as Truth the more likely it is the individual will continue on the path of discovery over the course of his or her existence.

While the awareness of Self exists on many levels across the cultures throughout your world, most do not encourage the Awareness we impart. The awareness required for the individual to assign his or her existence, in physical form, to the awe-inspiring curiosity required to explore this future is muted by its own existence.

Our observation with humankind has been that of consideration for the events leading to your evolution or comeuppance. Which we will tell you is very early in process, despite the generations of existence in form that have occurred.

The humanness of being requires parameters and measures to govern its processes. You, on the whole, are quite adept at creating processes, rules and regulations, units of measure, and criteria to be used for the discernment of things. The greatest buy-in from the masses, other than religion, is that of the units of measure related to the construct of time.

We agree demarcation helps you best function and advance technologically, physically, and intellectually (scientifically) while acquiring and maintaining some form of orderliness to these processes. Orderliness and control are areas for discussion at a later time. We tell you now, control, the concepts of exerting force, coercion to compliance over others, is also an illusion. More on this later as well.

For you to exist, such that you do presently, requires a blending of selves. Each of you makes this transition once human life begins in the womb of the identified human in which the life grows. We refer to the developing human as human, for that is what it is intended to be, just as a cow births cows and dogs birth dogs. The scientific distinctions for various stages of pre-birth development of the organism are not necessary for our teachings.

The human organism, on a cellular level, is a representation of all that it is to become. Each cell holds the information—DNA as identified by your sciences—necessary to continue replicating, ultimately developing the systems required by the whole to exist fully.

Within a specific period of human development, gestation, generally the eighth week after conception of life, the physical heart is complete and begins to function. Historically, when this organ was unable to perform, the human expired. Advances in technology now provide, for some, the opportunity to exist beyond its inability to perform optimally without intervention, thus offering an extended life experience.

At the moment of human conception is not when the Energetic Self fully occupies the physical form. While there is speculation by many regarding this process, we will tell you this. There is a knowing of the process and an awareness of the development of the physical form one is intended to occupy. That said, the heart is the indication of life for many, while life actually begins at conception.

Without all systems properly developed and fully functional, the organism cannot continue to exist. Such is the case when these processes are interrupted or otherwise do not complete, and the organism expires, resulting in what is known to you as miscarriage of the human form in development.

The development begins at conception. We say that is when life began. We acknowledge, however, the debate over this concept as it has grown to epic proportions more so now than any other period in your existence. While we are pleased consideration and a degree of reverence are given to human life, it is not extended to all life nor is consideration given to all life, such as it is with the physical. Even so, exploitation of human life exists.

While in development, before the birth, the physical form and the Energetic Self begin to become acquainted—one with the other. Experiences of Self are often not recollected or accounted for as the physical brain is in continual development throughout its pre-birth state. Therefore, remembrances and recollections of this time can be impressed upon the intellectual self as energetic imprints, and, of course, the post-birth state of awareness is better able to create this Reality once more reference material is acquired, through which the experience can be communicated.

The Energetic Self retains a record, and this record is accessible to some with integration through the physical systems, primarily the functions of the brain and the other energetic systems—the emotion and perception. In Reality, this information is accessible to all.

Truth of Being

Now, our Scribe wonders if these lessons are Truth in the way she regards information. To that, we say Yes. A resounding yes! She remains concerned about this information as it appears rudimentary, given the teachings she is aware of from others who also connect with Spirit or Source if you will (her words). We restate this information is as much for you, our Scribe, as it is to share with others who seek to learn, to awaken.

We will return to our former topic, the awareness process of Self and the physical form. To clarify one myth or misguided belief, the Energetic Self is in place, at least in part, at the time of physical birth.

Our Scribe is interrupting us now with concern she is somehow making up this information, to which we say, "So what if you are? Does it matter if your enlightenment comes from your inner wisdom or your consciousness?" She says a resounding yes! We say to that, your intent is commendable, and to query is good. Too much so impedes our processes. We honor your intellect and require challenge to ensure your curiosity is satisfied as these lessons unfold. As we have said, they are as much for you as anyone.

Now, birth has long been believed to be the point at which the Energetic Self enters the system. Some have been taught it is when the organism, baby, takes first breath. Our teachings ensure this is not the case and is, in fact, not factual. The two systems work to integrate during the developmental phases prior to the birth process.

We will also tell you there is a steep learning curve, as it were. Our energy, the energy of Self, is overlaid, if you will, on the processes of the physical form, which is also an electrochemical organism with processes of its own related to chemical substance transmitters and electrical impulses traveling throughout its varied pathways.

Our Scribe just envisioned the Self as a blanket of energy overlaid on the entire physical system, and she is only correct in part. The Self comes from within before it radiates or is emitted from the physical form. Then, it can be sensed, felt by many, as existing outside, around and shrouding the form. It comes from within.

So, what then in the event of a miscarriage or stillbirth, she asks? To that we say how should this process be any different for self? You are focusing on the aliveness or not aliveness of the physical. Soul is not physical and, therefore, has no life and death, such that form is subjected.

Rather, Self is infinite, expansive, endless. In the event of a malalignment of the physical form to maintain life prior to the birth process, Self does not change the interaction during the organism's development. There is still interaction between Self and the physical. Self does not require a conscious or intellect to experience, such that the awareness of Self requires in form; it is the same experience. The record of this interaction and involvement in a physical life becomes a part of the record of its experience.

When a malalignment occurs, as with a birth, the Self experiences not only its small self (physical form) but also the interactions with those around it. This is no different than if the Self inhabited the physical at the time of a live birth. Many are able to recollect, we say experience and report on, his or her gestation and birth in great detail. How could this occur if Self was not present during these processes, if Self was only present at the moment of physical birth or first breath? We say too that these are apples and oranges, indicating a misperception of Self and its interactions with the physical, especially pertaining to the development and birth of the human organism. Since we have brought forward information regarding the birth process and Self, we will also now speak to the death of the physical form and Self.

For the physical human organism, the process of death can be protracted and can take varying paths. It is not as if every individual is here one moment and suddenly not the next. However, we acknowledge that for many this is the case. In the event, at some point prior to its physical nonexistence, the organism contracts a threat or otherwise becomes afflicted, the Self is retained in part within the organism.

Similar to the development process, the death process, for lack of accurate terminology, is quite similar. However, we will say that during the development, Self is acclimating to form and relearning to integrate with such systems. During the deterioration of form, Self is reconnecting more fully with Universal Oneness. The individual may appear, at times, to be daydreaming, hallucinating (poor verbiage) in attempts to explain the unexplainable, or merely mentally unavailable. We say to you now this is not necessarily Truth.

The Self, during development, life, and now in the death process, is capable of existing within and separate from the form. Individuals are often more aware and at least better able to communicate these experiences as perceived and then reported due to consciousness awareness. Not uncommon are reports of an ill individual's awareness of activities with others or elsewhere than where the physical self is located, also known as projection of Self outside form. It is, however, more likely believed or entertained as Truth simply because the human self has been conditioned to find comfort in such things as a part of the death process.

We say this with the utmost love for the human process, the need to understand and to quantify and qualify experiences, although utilitarian, it impedes the death process by not affording time to the information brought forward and its Reverence and relevance to the individual, especially regarding existence of Self and its origins.

Instead, there is a comfort felt by those who want or need to experience the reuniting of Self with those who have gone before the one now before them in process of death. Yet, others explain away the revelations of the individual before them when the same utterings do not align with their belief system.

For us, it is a no-win situation, a Kobayashi Maru [rock and a hard place] interjected by our Scribe. Yes! This is exactly it. According to individuals, it is all very dichotomous. One way or the other, with no place for in-between or exploration of other Realities. In doing so, opportunities to learn are lost to those in witness of the death process.

A Message from The Collective Seven

Be kind to yourself, Dear One, as you practice living from your soul space. While it is your truest nature to live from the love that you are, aligning with your soul-self can be an emotional journey.

Awakening engages a heightened awareness and intensifies focus. You will begin to observe through a very different lens. Although viewing the world through the "eyes" of love is an enriching experience, it can be distressing to witness the unkindness imposed by your fellow humans upon each other, animals, and the planet.

Alignment with the soul-self naturally inspires those awakening to improve their manner of being in the world. Areas of focus include improvements to physical health and vitality through yoga, meditation, and spiritual practices; cleaner water, humanely raised animal food sources, vegetarianism, and veganism; a decrease or cessation of alcohol, caffeine, sugar, and tobacco consumption; and alternative forms of health care or increased interest in and use of herbal remedies and energy treatment methods versus pharmacological interventions.

Alternative lifestyles and activities are sought to diminish the negative planetary impact. For example, utilizing alternative heat and fuel sources, electric automobiles and limiting unnecessary travel, increasing recycling efforts, minimizing the use of nonrecyclable materials, eliminating products containing carcinogens or chemicals toxic to the individual and the environment, minimizing the carbon footprint, and living in an increasingly minimalistic manner.

Hopefully, by being stirred to research the areas mentioned above, you may develop personal love-inspired adaptations to your current ways of being. As you blend more fully into this lifestyle, the subtle changes will validate your chosen path.

For many, there is a deep yearning within and an almost insatiable desire to explore deeper and expand further. These individuals often become our global advocates for change by directly engaging in causes to address world hunger, climate change, preserving endangered species, the deinstitutionalization of caging wild animals (i.e., zoos, circuses), advocating to provide education and healthcare to the masses, and so on.

Be a catalyst for interpersonal change. Mirror the embodiment of love in all you do and to whomever you meet. If you desire to receive love, be love. Speak honestly to compel honest communication. Cultivate respect through respectful interactions. Compassion and loving-kindness are your soul's way. Shine your light for others to witness. Live from love, and you will receive that which you have given and more.

THE POWER OF YOUR PURPOSE

The soul is your internal guidance system, a compass that leads to its physical expression. Developing a conscious awareness of the self as a soul positions you to align with the love of your purpose. Alignment and complete integration of love, as intended, creates abundance and unparalleled gratitude for the experience of life. When you exist outside the subjectivity of a fear-based perspective, you can embrace everything as an essential part of the journey.

As a child, the consequences and rewards of your interactions with the world predominantly shape who you become. Equipped with an ability to intuit the energy of situations (i.e., people, animals, the environment), children are deeply connected with the properties of their energetic being. In fact, children are excellent messengers and examples of how to create and live a soul-centered life. Often identified as childhood innocence or naivete, the innate characteristics of a child—humble inquisitiveness, inclusive acceptance, altruistic kindness, and infinite benevolence—are the unabridged burgeoning soul self, present within us all at birth. A child aligned with their soul self who is supported and encouraged to live from this space possesses wisdom far beyond the combined years of his Earthly caregivers. These children flourish in ways never known to those constrained by society's expectations.

In the ebb and flow of life, discrepant energies create dissonance. It is difficult to exist and thrive when love is not the primary language of the words and actions one is exposed to. Children are often taught to disregard the energetic discomfort and adopt the expectations imposed upon them. To minimize the potential for consequences and to gain favor or approval, children comply at the expense of quelling the soul's voice. Forever changed, the soul self is disavowed little by little, often to the point where the soul's communications are no longer felt or heard.

Astute learners, children mimic and adopt the mannerisms, behaviors, and speech patterns modeled in their environment. So too, they learn to conform to expectations regarding gender, age, religion, and culture in addition to the expectations already reinforced through their interactions with caregivers, family, peers, and society in general.

In essence, a child learns to speak the language of their environment. Cognitive and behavioral shaping, used by civilizations throughout the world as standard child-rearing practice, occurs in many ways: modeling, positive reinforcement, coercion, manipulation, negative reinforcement (punishment or consequence), and physical force. The development of conformity and the disavowing of one's inner wisdom by any means further separates conscious awareness from the guidance of the soul.

Subdued by the experiences of life, the soul self tirelessly strives to emerge. Although metaphysical and spiritual practices have gained notoriety, children are not the only individuals to face negative appraisal for pursuing a connection with the soul self, outside the established and accepted societal norms. Despite its rise in popularity and contrary to notable benefits, the negative valuation of energy healing, spirit communications, and other such practices impacts those living from a place transcendent of the physical self. As a result, many adults choose to secret or deny altogether their conscious awareness of the soul self.

Raised in an environment of fear, void of the love and comfort a child craves, I learned as a very young child to straddle the fence of love and fear like an expert tightrope walker. It was not until many years, tears, and relationships later that I learned what love is and, more importantly, what love is not.

I learned for love to be as love's expression and experience are ultimately intended, it can only exist when led by acceptance of what is without expectation and unimpeded by judgment or valuation. My journey included acquiring knowledge through formal education and embracing my spirituality, which led to the release of everything that no longer served my best interest.

Admittedly, I feel like a phoenix who has risen from the ashes. Understandably, this creates a dramatic picture. Difficult to describe with mere words, the rebirth of the self is an extraordinary and powerful experience. To be love, I first had to acknowledge the love already within me, which required acceptance of the totality of my human (self) and the journey I had traveled to that point. Acceptance of myself as the embodiment of love and living consciously from love brought everything into balance and opened my life to the infinite abundance of love and gratitude available to us all.

Thankful to and for all who have shared in my journey and the many paths I have been blessed to walk; I have come to appreciate many things. Most importantly, I acknowledge the understanding of my purpose and accept that many others have not yet become consciously aware of the love of their soul self.

I also accept that those with whom we walk this journey are not always those with whom we begin it—this, too, is a part of the lived experience and the many lessons that unfold along the way. Nevertheless, I continue as a bridge between spirituality and the human condition to encourage others to discover their truth.

The quest for self is an enduring journey of discovery. My beliefs regarding our purpose—living from the love of the soul self and in harmony with others—transcend the limitations imposed by perspectives rooted in cultural norms, societal expectations, and subscribed religious or spiritual tenets. I encourage you to use this book as a starting point for exploring your way of being in the world. My hope for you is an enlightening path of self-discovery that leads you home.

> "Love is a state of Being. Your love is not outside; it is deep within you. You can never lose it, and it cannot leave you. It is not dependent on some other body, some external form. In the stillness of your presence, you can feel your own formless and timeless reality as the unmanifested life that animates your physical form. You can then feel the same life deep within every other human and every other creature. You look beyond the veil of form and separation. This is the realization of oneness. This is love."
>
> –Eckhart Tolle, *The Power of Now*

Acknowledgments

Love Is Unconditional is a vessel for truths that have been generously shared with me through the lived experience, and it would not have been possible without the collective wisdom and support of many.

I extend my deepest gratitude to my spiritual mentors, whose guidance has been a beacon throughout my journey. Your wisdom has shaped my path, and for this, I am forever thankful.

To the countless souls I have encountered through workshops and circle development, your insights and shared experiences have enriched this work immensely. Each interaction has been a precious thread in the fabric of this creation.

I am particularly grateful to Shanda Trofe and her wonderful team at Transcendent Publishing. Shanda, your belief in the power of spiritual narratives has given this book a home and a chance to reach the hearts of many. Your dedication to uplifting authors in the spiritual genre is an unwavering lighthouse for us all.

A special thanks to Mary Rembert, whose editorial insights have polished the raw expressions of my soul into the clear messages you find in these pages. Mary, your skill and dedication have truly elevated this work.

To my family and friends who have supported me through this process—your endless encouragement and belief in my vision have been pillars of strength.

Lastly, I want to acknowledge you, the reader, for embarking on this journey with me. This book is not just mine; it is a shared exploration of love and spiritual growth. May you find solace, inspiration, and love unconditional within its pages.

ABOUT THE AUTHOR

Shelley Love, Ph.D., is a licensed psychologist, intuitive, channel, and an explorer of human consciousness. With advanced education in clinical psychology and transpersonal spiritual practices, she brings nearly three decades of experience in harnessing science-based knowledge and consciousness investigations to deepen the understanding of our multifaceted existence.

Dr. Shelley serves as a voice for nonphysical energies, channeling their wisdom and messages to assist others in discovering their soul's purpose and transcending the limitations of their human experience. Known for her authenticity, candor, and unique ability to connect at a soul level, she facilitates transformative soul connections and channels spirit-led guidance that empowers individuals to confront and overcome their challenges.

A third-generation intuitive who has experienced spiritual phenomena from an early age, Dr. Shelley's childhood experiences profoundly enhanced her perceptual abilities and established lifelong direct communication with nonphysical entities. She is the creator of Soul Speak Meditation, a practice designed to foster self-discovery that offers insights into one's deepest inner knowing.

Deeply committed to the belief that living from our soul is crucial for humanity's ascension, Dr. Shelley advocates a shift from a competitive to a cooperative existence. She emphasizes the importance of maintaining a conscious awareness of Self to navigate life intentionally and with purpose.

Join Dr. Shelley Love in inspiring a global spiritual awakening as she guides you toward living your soul's purpose, embracing oneness, and enjoying the transformative journey of enlightenment.